STILLNESS

WITHIN THE

STORM

By Matthew Tolleth

Copyright © 2016, 2015 by Matthew Tolleth

Cover design by Julie & Dayna
Cover image: iStockPhoto, Royalty Free
Typography by Dayna Reid

All rights reserved.
No part of this book may be reproduced in any form or by any electronic or mechanical means including information storage and retrieval systems, without permission in writing from the author. The only exception is by a reviewer, who may quote short excerpts in a review.

Printed in the United States of America
First Printing: May 2015, Second Printing: August 2016

International Standard Book Number-13: 978-0997893809 (Softcover)
International Standard Book Number-10: 099789380X (Softcover)
Library of Congress Control Number: 2016912727

Published by Seattle Indie Press, Kent, WA
www.SeattleIndiePress.com

Visit the author's website at:
www.StillnessWithinTheStorm.com

To our four boys:

Matthew Jr.
Luke
Troy
Chase

Make your own guiding light to follow
for the life that you have chosen.
Make it bright and brilliant to guide your path.
Follow your heart and dreams.
Find time to play. Always!

Special Recognition

Julie, my bride to be. My moon, my stars, my everything. Thank you so very much for being patient with me these last few years while putting this project together. Thank you for pushing me forward, for calling me "out" when my direction wavered. Thank you for listening. Most of all, thank you for finding me.

Tim, my brother (and to his amazing betrothed "Snuggly"), my bulkhead and my Best Man to be. Best friends for almost 30 years. My thanks goes to you for striking up a two hour conversation in Key West, on how this project connected to you after reading the first unedited chapters. You are the first to realize the "exact" intention of my project.

To Boo, my friend for many years. You have the amazing ability to direct the focus of my thoughts and intentions—to move them forward without wandering. You are clear, understanding and articulate. This is what I give thanks for. This and a good many bottles of red wine we have shared. Plus you fit neatly in an overhead bin on an airplane—just saying.

For everyone else who joined in with me and read everything I have posted on social networks. Thank you all so much for being a part of this project! I am inspired by you!!

CONTENTS

Preface 1
INNER MISSION (An introduction too) 7

CHAPTER 1 11
The world is flat, right? 11

CHAPTER 2 19
Words, words and more words 19

CHAPTER 3 25
There is no "I" in Ego 25

CHAPTER 4 33
The illusionary world is all around us 33

CHAPTER 5 41
Let's go shopping! 41

CHAPTER 6 47
The Meaning of Life 47

CHAPTER 7 53
The past is what it is 53

CHAPTER 8 61
Quieting the mind 61

CHAPTER 9 67
Look through me and you will know me 67

CHAPTER 10 75
Life is short, live it while you can 75

CHAPTER 11 81
Your Life 81

CHAPTER 12 91
The Human Condition 91

CHAPTER 13 99
Shared Box Theory 99

CHAPTER 14 105
Of Sticks and Stones 105

CHAPTER 15	**111**
THIS TOO SHALL PASS	111
CHAPTER 16	**115**
OF LIGHT AND DARK	115
CHAPTER 17	**121**
THE DESIGNER DISORDER OF THE DAY	121
CHAPTER 18	**127**
ANTIDEPRESSANTS	127
CHAPTER 19	**133**
YOU MAKE ME FEEL	133
CHAPTER 20	**137**
IT IS, WHAT IT IS	137
CHAPTER 21	**141**
START DEFINING WHAT IS IMPORTANT TO YOU	141
CHAPTER 22	**145**
IS IT DIET TIME FOR YOUR EGO?	145
CHAPTER 23	**151**
CHANGE YOUR THOUGHTS, CHANGE YOUR LIFE	151
FINAL THOUGHTS	**153**
ENDING NOTE	**155**
ABOUT THE AUTHOR	**157**

Preface

Disclaimer and Caution: Why are you reading this and why am I writing this?

First of all, I don't know why you are reading this. Secondly, I enjoy sharing the workings of my mind (which is a very scary place). These writings can be compared with reading an Oracle. When I say Oracle, the meaning I want to convey is that within this work, you will find what speaks to you and your life—past, present, and future.

I'm writing this to connect the dots. This is what I do best. The dots being, what I've learned through reading a book here, a magazine article there, and by wandering the world, making a game out of watching and listening to people. Just like tumblers in a lock, eventually, ideas click into place for me, and new ideas are created and connected.

Assuredly, there are areas within these pages that will connect with you. Some of the writing you will completely disagree with and some will be unnerving at times, while other times you will get that proverbial light that switches on. I am going to dig at the very truths that you hold true, and I'm going to help you challenge them. There are no right or wrong answers here—no finite answer in what I want to convey. Regardless, I suggest/hope that you will keep reading.

I have no hidden agenda. I hold no religious affiliation to be the total or ultimate truth. The institution of religion or organized religion used to scare the crap out of me, but I've found peace with this. Believing in a higher power and spiritual teachers no longer frightens me—a higher power can be a good thing when it's in the hands of kind people with honest intentions. Believing in and witnessing the kind actions of others strengthens my resolve when I'm surrounded by the dark behavior of others that seems to cast a shadow upon the light of the kindhearted.

Life can feel overwhelming—fast and complicated. We cannot wipe from our memories what we have seen. Our daily news is full of suffering and emphasizes the vileness of what we're capable of as a race in the past and present.

One question I want to present you with is: Why is this one-sided perspective promoted in our daily life and what elements affect what you see and hear every day?

Having an open mind and the willingness to accept new ideas (not implying in any way that you don't) wouldn't hurt. Here, you will find something useful. If you have disagreements with the ideas that I present (and you will) the argument will be within the duality of yourself. I will be unbalancing the world as you see it, and the ideas I present can rip that world apart. This can be very upsetting at times (to say the least). My goal is to start the thinking process and spark a few ideas that may lead you to discover new depth within yourself.

This is just the start, and it's not an easy road to travel. This is more of an enlightenment of the mind, body and soul.

There is no personal goal for you to achieve here—and you needn't seek one. As I stated earlier, my goal with this book, is to simply create that one "spark" to ignite that "something" within you to look at your life differently.

At some point in our life, we try to re-invent ourselves. I caution you to NOT attempt this. We don't need to re-invent ourselves, but only discover the illusion and what role it has played in our life. With this discovery there will be many questions. And I urge you to continue to educate yourself and keep learning.

An illusionary life resides in each of us, overshadowing the quiet mind and life we're really living.

The writing within this book does have concept-generating and thought-provoking ideas around "stillness" and the idea of "stillness" within the "storm." My intention with the use of the word "stillness" is to help you discover and create a comfortable reality where you are not influenced by thoughts other than those of your personal choosing and where you make the choices that are best for you. My hope with this project is that you will break that barrier, that subliminal influence. And you will find a new world of choices, choices that move with you as you move your way through this mess we call existence—through the "storm" of your life.

Preface

At the very least, I hope to be thought-provoking enough to help you keep reading and seeking what speaks to you.

I believe this writing transcends the physical, so allow me to postulate on the reason why this book may have captured your attention. I can only explain my own discoveries and reasoning. When I began this journey, I would walk through a bookstore and books would almost jump into my hands. Not physically mind you. It was more of a gravitation or friendly push or urge (sorry, it is difficult to explain).

I can only speculate that one of the reasons you're reading this is because you feel like you're on the edge of drowning, trying to catch your breath while water keeps splashing you in the face (that is how I felt at times). Or maybe not. Maybe you have a different reason. With all reasons aside, you are here, now.

I can tell you, before this writing, there came a time when I was just tired of always feeling awful. The mental aspects of my life at the time spilled over and physically made me feel ill, sick, and in pain.

It has been a very long road for me indeed! Well not so much a long road, but more like a long tumble down an embankment, all the while yelling, "That didn't hurt!" at every bounce. As you can see, I was in denial. It was painful!

When I finally landed I was out of breath! I remember that there was a lot of pain. It was definitely a bottom for me and I could clearly see there was more distance to travel downward. Yet I couldn't see into the darkness below me. Although I did land on a ledge and my foot was caught and pinned me in place. I could see the unending abyss over the ledge and the claw marks of others who were not so lucky, drifting down and over the edge into the abyss. What a scary thought and how lucky I felt at this break—caught between and given the chance to take a healing breath.

At times, I glance back at my own path that led to my fall. I'm not proud of that path mind you, and I understand the cascading effects of the options that were presented to me at the time. On this ledge, stuck between—I discovered that; the past cannot be changed, altered, or even made amends for. The past is what it is … Just that. What is important then? The here and now! This is what defines you as you segue from one moment to the next. When this idea finally hits you, you will find there is little or no value in dwelling on past events.

Our existence seems to be filled with so much hatred and misery that even tiny reprieves of happiness dissolve as quickly as they are experienced—like catching a snowflake.

No worries. This book will question your thoughts and help spark some wonderful ideas to help you extinguish the surrounding negativity you live within. If you don't live in any negativity, hey good for you ... You really don't need this book so please put it down and pass it on to someone else. Suggest it to a friend that could use some reassurance. If you do need this message, if you feel the need to share this message, please read on and share what you've learned with others.

You have nothing to lose with the suggestions I will present and everything to gain! Here's a sample ...

First and foremost, I want you to learn to use the "mute" button on your remote. I want you to discover how much time is spent watching commercials versus watching your chosen programming. Soon you will discover that you are watching commercials more than your programming.

Next, turn the radio off in your car and put on music that is uplifting to you. Most of the content on cable and the radio is psychologically engineered to keep you listening and watching no matter what the subject content is. If you want to see for yourself, get a stopwatch or timer and calculate the difference between program time and commercial time. I think this would surprise you.

What should really surprise you is that you're paying someone to psychologically convince you to buy something that you don't really need!

This is the best cost-benefit suggestion that I could ever provide for you. And it will put money back into your pocket to provide for you and or your family!

The satellite and cable companies are not going to like me telling you this. Your family and your children are not going to like this either. So, if you must have your TV, there are inexpensive internet-to-TV (flat screen) options that cost less than 30 cents a day.

Preface

When I finally dumped commercialized cable TV, I discovered that I was not alone! I discovered friends in my social network—old friends and new had done the same. We started connecting with each other and sharing stories about the desire to distance ourselves away from commercialization and more.

Take this challenge and start muting commercials. Do this for 30 days or more. It takes about 21 days to form a new habit.

Throughout this book, I'll be systematically offering you suggestions to improve your state of being. These first suggestions were easy and simple to undertake. There is little or no risk to you. And I want you to understand that the challenges I present will become more difficult and more challenging to undertake, not only for you, but also for those around you. Time to fasten your seat belts. Put your tray table in the upright and locked position. This just might be a bumpy ride! :-)

Just one last thing:

The best lessons I've ever learned are those I've stumbled upon on my own. Others can tell us of their experiences. Yes, those are nice stories. And yes, we can learn from those stories—but we are disconnected from the experience.

We can hear, "Be careful, your plate is hot!" But, until we place our hand on that plate and feel the searing pain, there is message is incomplete. One reason for this is that we have to experience it for ourselves. Once we experience the direct pain involved, we'll finally "connect the dots" and comprehend the intended message.

I hope to write in a way that will move you to that moment of discovery without the pain. This can be an impossible task. The best I can hope or you is; to get you to the point where when I tell you something is hot—you pause and *feel* the heat rise before you engage.

I won't necessarily explain all my talking points. This is done on purpose. I want you to discover the message on your own and how it applies to your existence—not mine. I want you to read a sentence and ask questions about it and seek the answer that best fits you. You will find that I can word sentences in a manner that you will have to stop and re-read them several times. If I explained everything to you in my writing, so you completely understood, it would be patronizing—and more like a 12-step program.

So, relax and read. This is your own path to discovery. Please don't ask me to spoil the surprise of the learning experience for you.

INNER MISSION
(An introduction too)

Welcome to "Inner Mission." Before you read Chapter One, I want to give you a "heads-up" on the chapters you are about to read.

When we pick apart "Stillness within the Storm," the element of the "storm" is persistent and prevalent in our lives today. We need to be comfortable with the state of our life as we currently see it. Let me stress this point; I'm not telling you to "like" it, I'm suggesting that you accept it as it is.

"Stillness" represents a feeling of contentment within you. This is a subjective feeling and/or emotion—it is revealed differently in each of us. The "storm" on the other hand, represents your current life and the way you think and live. What do we want to accomplish here? We are looking to create a space between you and the world that exists around you.

The following chapters will peel back the layers of our human condition and expose them to you. Similar to peeling an onion, with every layer we peel back, come tears.

Within our DNA, life's darkness can be captivating at times—and I'm speculating here—because the universe is trying to teach us a lesson. I don't know what the lesson is; it is different to each of us. But for the purposes of this book, I'm going to gravitate toward: "learning acceptance."

Once we achieve the "acceptance" part of life that is around us, that is when an element within us expands. Once it expands large enough, the storm of life starts to move around us instead of moving through us.

Before we begin, here are some terms that we will use throughout the book and the meaning with which we will use them:

Consciousness: Awareness at the present moment. Your awareness of things both outside you as well as mental functions happening on the inside.

Subconscious: Consists of accessible information in the mind, which you are not currently aware of. You can become aware of this information once you direct your attention to it. Think of this as memory recall. For example, you can drive to your house without consciously needing to remember the route. But you can easily bring to consciousness the subconscious information about the path to your home.

Ego: the self of an individual person; the conscious subject. One's image of one's self.

Unconscious: the part of the mind that is inaccessible to the conscious mind but that affects behavior and emotions. We don't have easy access to the information stored in the unconscious mind. During our childhood, we acquired countless memories and experiences that formed who we are today. However, we cannot recall most of those memories. They are unconscious forces (beliefs, patterns, subjective maps of reality) that drive our behaviors.

An "Inner Mission" will precede each chapter and offer tasks for you to participate in. I truly hope you engage in these activities. This will help your experience with this book be much more gratifying. We all learn in different ways. So, find what works best for you.

At the end of each "Inner Mission" will be a "Stillness For Thought," a quote or thought to help you contemplate the lesson covered in the Inner Mission.

Let's get started!

INNER MISSION
(An introduction too)

Stress, anxiety and fear in our current daily lives are caused by our overactive ego, thinking of situations *that have not happened!* I cannot stress enough the importance of this; **stress, anxiety and/or fear that has NOT happened!** It is all about the overactive ego. You will discover more as you read on.

FEAR can also be defined as: *F*alse *E*motions *A*ppearing *R*eal. Keep this acronym in mind as you read on.

Stillness For Thought:

God, grant me the serenity
to accept the things I cannot change,
The courage to change the things I can,
And the wisdom to know the difference. (The Serenity Prayer)

Stillness Within the Storm

Chapter 1

The world is flat, right?

Is this the truth? There was a time in our history that the "powers that be" (academics, leaders of faith, scholars and politicians), were all in agreement and discerned that the world was flat and declared it thus. If you sailed far enough out to sea, you would just drop off the edge of the earth. Perceptually, the earth under us does look flat when we look around. But, this is only an illusion. If you were on a boat out to sea, the farthest you could see is fourteen miles due to the natural curvature of the earth. It looks flat, so it must be flat.

During this time in history, we believed that if we sailed far enough out to sea we would just drop off into the abyss—off into the end of the world. This was a *belief*. It became the truth and was accepted as fact for many years. It was a foundational reality. Something rock solid validated by the "powers that be."

Just imagine how difficult it was for Columbus to convince the "powers that be" that the earth was round? How challenging was it for Galileo to prove that the earth was not the center of the universe? Imagine the personal sacrifice he had to endure to prove his point.

The sun, moon, and stars appear to move around us. Therefore, we must be the center of it all—the center of the universe. It seems logical, but given enough time, the strong beliefs that we hold close, that we hold so unwaveringly true, can ultimately, change. To further this point, the world is *not* flat and the Earth is *not* the center of the universe. It was simply the strong *belief* that the Earth was flat and the center of the universe.

Another example from history is, "It was on day four that God created the sun, moon and stars to embellish earth with light." Anyone who said differently? Imprisoned. This belief and punishment for disagreement about this, thus defying the Bible continued for many years. But was the battle over truth, idealism, the Holy Scripture, or clashing personalities?

Speaking out against a group or righteous individual's beliefs has had devastating effects on personal health and well-being of many. Let's look at Copernicus as one example as we look back through history—heresy, trials, imprisonment and executions solely based on holding a different outlook, an alternate point of view. The devastation inflicted, especially by those whose egos were so massive and powerful within them (self-rightness) that it reached to the sky—even to the heavens. Copernicus' publication, *On the Revolution of the Celestial Spheres,* was not published until after he passed. He knew enough about the human condition to realize that he would be hunted down and imprisoned if he went against the church with his discovery.

Within the clash, conflict, and disagreements of the egos of people from the past, self-rightness has determined the best path for everyone. These same people burned books and made people disappear, thus erasing history to protect their own beliefs of right and wrong—to protect *their own* egos. The loss due to these disagreements of the ego has been devastating to us all. The ego supports and protects the foundation of our beliefs, even when those beliefs are wrong.

To discover how big of a role your Ego plays in your beliefs, here are some important questions to ask yourself:

How many times have you thought something to be true and later found out it wasn't true?

How many times have you argued a belief that you held and in time, changed your mind?

How many times have you been in arguments, yelling and screaming until you were blue in the face only to find out that the argument had no basis in truth?

How many times have you argued a point where you were given solid physical proof of being wrong but still held your ground?

I don't want you to get the idea that I believe that the way I think is better than anyone else's way of thinking. Because it's not. I'm just another guy. At times, I've held on to my convictions even though I was blatantly proven wrong. Been there, done that. The ego supports our foundation of beliefs to protect our zone of comfort, and it doesn't like to be wrong. Being wrong diminishes us and our sense of self. The ego will fight for its beliefs even though the perceived truth is not so true after all.

Why do we feel the need to be "better than?" Individuals in humankind strive to be "better than." It's our nature. Understanding and realizing this is a key point. We feel larger than life when we're right. When we're wrong, we feel as if a part of us has been unfairly dissected from who we believe we are, and we feel smaller, and we feel loss.

If you aren't "better than," then what are you ... If you were without an ego, who would you be?

This is an important question you must ask yourself. In the chaos of our present life, in the mixture of information overload, with all the buzz and distractions of everything around us—the idea of the present moment is lost. We have others trying to influence how we think, how we shop, what we should buy, how we should live, what we should think is important, who we should vote for, what beliefs are righteous and should be followed, how we should act, who we should marry, what our life should look like, what car we should drive, how much money we should make, and how much better we would look if we bought thus-and-such. The simple act of contemplating "how to be better than" strengthens the ego. Ego becomes larger when we tune or align ourselves to a grander idea.

Life is fluid and ever-changing, like a stream that flows from the high mountains downward through the forest and fertile valleys. Every element of life that the water touches changes with it, including the life that it supports from microorganisms that live within it, helping to regulate the earth itself. Even solid rock will eventually dissolve into the stream, providing trace minerals to support even more life in this way. I say life is fluid and ever-changing because nothing, absolutely nothing is permanent. Even the values and truths that we hold so true contain a wavering fluidness within them. Sometimes our core beliefs are so solid we associate them with a rock. This metaphor demonstrates the unmoving and everlasting perceived evidence that a belief will always be there. But, is this the truth?

As the slogan says, "Like a rock, your insurance company will always be there."

"My family is a rock that I know will always be there for me—I can count on them."

Companies use this belief to sell their goods because all of us have some association with a rock representing permanency in life—something that will always be there, and we all know it. And yet, is a rock really a permanent structure? Is it unchanging like so many other ideas that we hold true? Our truth, our beliefs can be just as solid as a rock. The more people that agree with us, the stronger the belief becomes. It becomes true and right. It can't be wrong because many other people share our belief. It reaches the level of being right or wrong, truth or untruth. But, under enough pressure and heat, a rock can change form—like the rivers of lava that flow from Kilauea in Hawaii. There is nothing that can't be changed. Given enough time, enough heat and pressure, all things change in time.

We desire and need to believe in an ultimate truth. Humankind needs to feel grounded—to feel some kind of security within them. Ultimate truths provide a blanket effect. The bigger the blanket (ultimate truth) that covers a group of people, the more likely there is to be a warm and fuzzy feeling shared through a commonality of experience and agreement.

In the previous example of the belief that the world is flat, one person was tugging on the edge of the blanket threatening to destabilize the ground and let in the cold harsh air of reality, dissolving the foundation of the belief. Believing in ultimate truths can blind us to the point where we only look in one direction. This effect can have devastating consequences when taking the stance that one thing is right and one thing is wrong with no middle ground—black or white with no option for gray or alternative understandings. The truth as it seems is not the truth at all, but, merely an illusion of the word, *truth*. We use this word to provide foundation and stability—to feel comfortable. It's difficult to live our lives without believing in some truth to feel secure and safe. We feel uncomfortable when our truth becomes ungrounded. Our egos thrive on focusing on the difference between right and wrong and use the truth or the illusion of truth to validate our belief. Life is fluid, free flowing, and ever-changing in form, moment by moment. Change is all around us whether we accept it or not.

INNER MISSION

They say it takes about 21 days to form a habit. And this is what you will be doing while participating in each "Inner Mission." Follow the directions given for 21 consecutive days and see what happens!

Your first task will be to keep a daily, written journal. During each chapter, write in this journal any thought or feeling that comes into your mind. There is no expectation of what the content should be. Just let your mind wander and let the words flow.

To begin to address the over-activity of our mind, we first have to reduce the visual waste that contributes to it.
Your mission is twofold:

When you watch cable TV, pick up the remote and mute the commercials. I want you to observe the amount of time your program plays versus the commercial time you are made to watch. Write your discoveries in your journal each day as you engage in this activity.

Next?

Clear and organize your environment: Your bedroom, bathroom, home, car, and work space. Your mission? Box up everything that you don't use on a daily basis. All non-essential clutter will be gone and packed up neatly into boxes and stored out of view. Next, new cozy sheets for your bed, new socks and underwear. Find what helps you feel good inside. Dishes are cleaned when they are dirtied. Clothes thrown in the washer-dried then folded and put away. Bed made every morning.

If something is broke, fix it or throw it away!

Your vehicle will be free of clutter, washed, waxed, vacuumed and get an oil change! It doesn't matter what year or what shape it is in.

Every non-essential item in your home will be packed away. Leave artful pieces that bring joy into your life where they may be visible. Empty your junk drawers into a box and use the extra space to put away something that you use daily. Again, I am not suggesting you throw these things away.

As with your home life, we will do the same with your work life. Keep in sight, only what is necessary to the job at hand.

Visual clutter doesn't bring joy into your life. Studies have shown that when you take an active role in the environment around you, only good can come from this positive action.

Stillness For Thought:

Open your mind to the wonderful world of everything around you. Feel the earth under your feet as you walk. Feel the touch of the wind upon your face. Stop and let the world fill your senses.

Stillness Within the Storm

Chapter 2
Words, words and more words

I know I've tossed around the word ego quite a few times in the first chapter and there is a reason for this. Be patient with me. There is a method to my madness. Words are ever-changing and ever-changing us. Our current language over the centuries has been translated and retranslated over and over, throughout time. Within those translated words are lost meanings. Not only lost meanings, but also lost feelings associated with those meanings in context.

There have been those in the past who have changed the course of the future by omitting or destroying important historical elements that were especially important for those in the future. An example of this is the recent discovery of the existence of the Gospel of *Judas*.

If you take the time to dig, really dig ... you will discover that the word Gospel, accurately translated, means, "to bring or announce good news, or messenger of good news." From historians we learn that there were over thirty Gospels and only the most popular four made it into the New Testament of the Bible: Matthew, Mark, Luke and John written by anonymous authors over 60 years later. There were no formal churches and the spreading of the *"good news"* was accomplished by people from their homes.

Throughout time we have changed the meaning of our words to conform to current trends and reflect the atmosphere of our thoughts and feelings at a societal level. Those who have held the power of persuasion have held the power over history. The destruction or exclusion of *lost* Gospels is a good example of this idealism.

Here are some other current examples of how word meanings have evolved:

> **Ejaculate**: Today this word is used in association with the ending feature of copulation. While years ago it was used in literary form to describe verbal expression without pre-thought (in other words, to not "think before you speak")—to throw out, or eject.
>
> **Retarded**: Today this word has become a derogatory term used to refer to people who suffer from Down's syndrome or other physical or mental challenges. But, this word simply means: turned back or slowed. Look at an automotive repair manual and you will find directions on how to *retard* the timing of your engine.

These two words have changed form just within the last fifty years or so and aren't used in casual conversations because of the stigma behind them. As time passes, terms and phrases are quickly being shoved into the "words to *never* be used again" category.

So how has the translation of words over the past 100 to 1000 years changed our language today? How obscure and muddled have our words become? When we think of snow, we think of falling, fluffy, frozen, flakes that are fun to play in. We think of the possibility of a snow day from school (kids' version). Adults think about the physical labor and stress involved in getting to work. We call it *snow*. But, did you know that the Eskimo have fifteen distinct words for snow? Words that mean: snowflake, to snow, fine snow, drifting snow, etc.

How does this language evolution affect us today?

In 2011 alone, there were 10 new words added to the Oxford English Dictionary, reflecting the fluidness of words in current times. This gives promise that we are adaptable to change.

We have a tendency to categorize our words and all their meanings into a neat, tidy, segregated box so that it's easy to listen to conversations and pick the right word from the box then move on. It is like a Bento box of Japanese cuisine. In each section is content, presentation, body language, context, meaning, possible meaning, non-verbal's alternative meaning and my favorite: the grab bag (this is when you give an understanding nod to a comment and later discover the real meaning of that comment).

How often do we overlook another's body language and just accept the presentation and definition because the body language and feeling of the message requires too much effort to discern?

Words also have the ability to add to or take away from the significance, feeling, and meaning of anything they describe. For example, what really happened in history? We have no other choice but to understand ancient history as the translators and writers have depicted it. And who chooses what is to be remembered and what is not to be remembered? Is our ancient history forever muddled, misleading and lost? I think not. Humankind is endlessly curious about anything and everything. Give us enough time and we will continue to discover new elements of everything.

Even if we use words to describe a positive action, we will often negate the good elements of what we are trying to express. Let me explain further. What is the difference between using *battle* or *war* in a positive way? A victor in *battle* can be easily ascertained. We can comprehend who the victor is numerically by counting the people left standing. Battle is a physical means of determining the outcome. When we use *war*, we are looking at the strategic aspect of battle that is fuzzy in determining who the victor is.

Both *battle* and *war* include the negative aspect of the extinguishing of life in the process of winning or losing. Battles have been won, and what was the cost? Wars are never won. They just lay dormant and reignite in a different way later. Battle and war are two examples of highly volatile words that never should be used while addressing and promoting positive change. How long have we had a *war on drugs*? "Drugs" is a neutral word relating to pharmaceuticals. There will be no clear victor in this fight. The *war on drugs* just supplies the people who *war* with more money to do so—we all lose!

With moving pictures and recording devices and their continued improvement, we get closer to understanding history more accurately. We have documentaries that are narrated while a recording device puts us right in the action like we are experiencing it as it is happening. We are coming into an age of understanding.

One important thing to think about: nothing is ever as it seems. All of us see, feel, and communicate things differently. The written language is ever-changing in significance, feeling, and meaning. And sometimes in rare instances, we can discover something new about ourselves through better understanding; how we operate, how we relate to our existence, and how we determine who we think we are.

INNER MISSION

As you are currently addressing your external distractions we are going to address the internal ones too.

Find a small note pad with pages that can be easily ripped out.

Your mission? Write down any past "indiscretions" that come to mind. Some may call it a "wrong" that has never been "righted." Some may even call it a "sin or sinful act." I also want you to write down every regret you have ever had.

Each indiscretion or regret will be written down on a single piece of paper and folded in half. This will be an ongoing activity until all are accounted for.

Now, find a safe place to light a fire. A ***very safe place*** to light a small fire.

In this safe place to light a fire, take your folded piece of paper with your indiscretion or regret on it and carefully light it on fire. (Did I say find a "safe place to light a fire" enough times?)

This exercise will release your indiscretion or regret back into the universe; it is no longer yours to own now. The universe will deal with it as it chooses. Everything changes in form and context when it moves within our existence. In our "human condition" we know the power of releasing our indiscretions and or regrets, because it is so hard for us to let go of the past. The exercise I just presented to you is ancient, and it is still used by many today. Catholics call it "confession."

In the next few chapters, your reading will expose your ego. It is not unlike exposing a raw nerve. You will feel the emotion of anger. Remember that the "ego" does not want to be discovered. The anger you feel is a natural process. Don't suppress it. Allow it to breathe and watch how it takes control and exists. Write about it. Explore it.

Stillness For Thought:

Many of us can get "stuck" thinking about events that have happened in the past. So much so that it makes us question our very existence. We are not defined by our past.

My question to you is: If the past were no longer important to you, how would this change your life today?

Chapter 3

There is no "I" in Ego

As strange as it may sound, there is an "I" in Ego. Let me explain. We use "I" in descriptive form when we're talking about ourselves in conversation. "*I* woke up this morning and guess what happened?" "*I* stood in line for hours just so *I* could be one of the first people to purchase the next new phone." "I" is closely associated with: me, my, and mine. "I" is also used in the possessive form to express the feeling of ownership; we talk of "I" then follow it up with what we did or what we own. We are wandering around in a world of "I," "me," "my," and "mine." We love to talk about ourselves. We love to talk about what we have and what we own. And the person we are talking with relates to this form of expression and can't wait to sing their own praises. And the cycle continues. This just is.

"I" is the simplest of the one-letter words in the English language. But, this simple letter is ginormous (another new word that has been added to our language recently). "I," when translated from Latin into English, means: "ego." In conversation, each of us has our own special categorized bento box of meaning for the word ego (we talked about this in the last chapter). We all grasp what it means. We draw from our bento box and move on with the conversation.

But, what is the ego? In the academic world, the ego has been picked apart, analyzed and sorted into categories. Countless educators and scholars have spent their whole life dissecting this word. Case studies and papers describe what it is and the effects of it on our lives.

You can study the "ego", the "super-ego," and the "id." This is all great progress. But, how many educators help you to actually identify the ego within yourself? Where is it? Can you feel it? Can you touch it? Where is it hidden?

The ego is elusive. It doesn't want you to know that it exists within you. Because in its discovery, lies its possible end. It will do anything and everything in its power to prevent this! You can find and identify with your own ego just by listening. It is that voice inside your head that continues talking. And it does so endlessly! The voice that prevents you from going to sleep at night, talking about the day's events and how to prepare for tomorrow—The voice that reaches into your past and brings up conflicts, hurt, and pain—The voice that reaches into the future, causing anxiety, wondering what you will do next. It talks and talks and talks… The only place it doesn't have any power over you is in the present moment.

Most of the world lives unconsciously in an egotist state. You could say that we are parasites upon this earth—the home that supports us and our livelihood. We don't give back, and we take, use and waste. We are not symbiotic and we use until there is no more. But, this doesn't mean that we are intentionally destructive.

We're in the discovery stage of learning about all of the harm we have caused and continue to cause to our environment—and it may be too late to fix. Globally, we're still that 2-year-old child grabbing at the one toy that another is holding, shouting, "Mine!" You give that child (us) what he wants and you pick up another toy and the other child's response, while putting down his current toy is to reach out again and say, "Mine!" This is our *storm*. This is our unconscious, egotist state that the storm is created from.

A good progression from this first point of ego discovery is to begin to recognize who you really are. That is, if you make it through the transition of realizing the duality of yourself—who you are, versus whom your ego has created. And understand this one important part: your ego doesn't want to be discovered. It doesn't want to be sought after. It doesn't want to be hunted. If you intentionally seek it, it will by order of self-preservation, sidetrack you by creating a new and better you. Don't fall for this deception. It's just a different mask to create, a new element of your ego to construct to keep you from awareness.

For those of you who decide to take the time to intentionally seek out your ego, please join our community on the website (www.stillnesswithinthestorm.com) or on Facebook and feel free to post and share your work. This is a good way for all of us to gain a better understanding of our progression.

From personal experience, the ego diminishes to almost nothing when it has nothing left—when all is gone or taken away. When we've lost everything important to us—everything that made us who thought we were—everything that we ever wanted, taken away for whatever reason. When we are left with nothing, the ego goes into hibernation. It leaves us too.

Hibernation? Yes, when the ego has nothing left to feed itself, it hibernates. But, the ego knows that given enough time, there will be food.

At this point, what remains are two paths.

Discovering the duality of yourself or nothingness.

Nothingness is just that—an absence of all. You can find it everywhere. Kind souls do their best to help others in this vast wasteland. You can observe this nothingness on park benches covered in newspaper—sleeping on the sidewalk—homeless people pushed aside. In some, you can witness when the nothingness grabs hold and the ego crosses over the line from mindful to verbal. Most of us become uncomfortable around those lost people when they endlessly babble, openly talking to no one in particular. Why do we feel uncomfortable?

Maybe on an underlying level, we recognize that our ego doesn't want itself to be discovered either.

On the opposite end of the spectrum, the nothingness just slips away on a cold evening—tagged in the morgue as John or Jane Doe—lost to some, lost to no one …

Our ego can be our worst enemy at times. It really doesn't care for its host. It has no conception that if its host is no longer, it will be no longer.

The awareness of ego, its unearthing, only emerges through self-discovery, ultimate personal loss, or at times by accident. Who are you? How does the ego answer this question? Many of us have focused a lifetime on "who am I" based on our life's work and profession. The ego takes on the label—doctor, father, plumber, mechanic, wife, salesman, etc.—and defines who we are based on who others think we should be.

We can become so devastated by a situation or by words or actions of another that our ego gets crushed and damages the very health of the biological entity that is supporting our ego.

When your ego has been injured in any way, it won't allow you to stop thinking about the injury causing circumstances. It plans—it schemes.

The first thing to notice when your ego's foundation has been discovered is *denial*. Especially when the Ego's foundation is revealed, there's a burst of raw anger—you "see red." This doesn't last long and your ego is quick to misdirect your thoughts.

Most important to understand is that we're identifying, as we communicate with others, an element that has been created over our years living in a false sense of self. We're all amazing, living, breathing, walking, entities—beautiful incarnations capable of much love and compassion. And, at the same time capable of copious evil and destruction. The ideas presented here are not new and are not lost. They are hidden from you within an element of yourself.

Here are some closing thoughts as we conclude this chapter that will help transition you for what comes next:

I was looking for a way to describe the ego-focused Western world we live in and no one word could explain the intent and magnitude of what I wanted to express to you, my reader. Since I have no academia or credentials to back my writings, I quickly find my limits are endless. And I love this!

Egotic is the new word I put together using two different word parts; *ego* and *otic*. We have a concept of what ego means—otic, on the other hand, is Greek in its origin and is used following a noun. It describes a state between the two word parts in action, state, condition or process. So, put together, we have, "the Ego condition" or "state of being Ego."

Believe it or not, ego is a noun! It's, a person, place or thing as described in the dictionary.

Wow, that worked out better than I thought. *Ego* a noun, and *otic,* following a noun, fits perfectly. But is *ego,* a person or thing? I can see both here. It's definitely not a place, or is it? Could it be … all three?

Let me present two ideas and one statement. Maybe the ego is a state of mind that we (and others have contributed to) and have created throughout our lifetime. A collective existence. And maybe there is an underlying element—a part of us that is unconscious and aware. This is the duality of us that I mentioned in the last chapter and there seems to be more; the idea that the subconscious is also lingering behind the curtains in our minds.

Now here is your statement:

Your ego is an abstract part of who you are. The dictionary defines "ego" as a noun. And not any ordinary noun, it is an abstract noun. An abstract noun is something you can't feel, taste, touch, see, or hear. And defining the word abstract? It is considered apart from concrete existence. A concrete existence is a tangible existence. So we are one step closer to discovering our illusionary life. Please stay tuned.

Now, let's attach the concept that our ego is our predominate and current conscious state of mind. Read this definition and see how well it fits:

Egotic:

An action, process, state, or condition related to the ego in excess with emphasis on self-importance, with little or no regard for the consequential sequence of time, space, causality; and a blatant disregard of effectual means of communication with self and others. Synonym: sociopath.

To plainly describe this term, think of the concept, self-centered. In the extreme, we see actors and singers that are in the news every day; people who are breaking down to the point that they cut off all their hair or are in a constant transition between rehabilitation centers and courtrooms. The strangest part about this; many of us *want* to watch this self-centeredness in action. This tells us a lot about the illusion we are living.

As soon as you start paying attention to the voice(s) in your head, you start dissolving your illusionary life. And you start understanding the difference between you and your ego. This is a very important aspect of moving you from where you are now toward understanding the significance of recognizing what is before you.

So… One more time with feeling!

As soon as you start **listening** *to the voice(s) in your head you start dissolving your illusionary life. And you start understanding the difference between you and your ego.*

Soon, you will be watching your ego at work and as you do this, you will begin to understand that there is another part of you underlining your ego. This is not your ego—this is the real YOU!

Other games to play that help you understand the mechanisms at work here are fairly simple.

Try going a whole day without using the words: I, me, or mine.

When I tell you that your life is just an illusion... How do you feel? And how do you feel when I tell you that your illusionary life is self-created?

INNER MISSION

The next chapter will begin to talk about your duality. Understand that it may anger you at times to expose your ego in its raw state and form. Take comfort in the idea that it is not really who you are. A damaged ego is not visible in our physical element, and it doesn't have the ability to cause physical harm (unless it controls you and makes you act out of anger).

During your average day, become aware of how many times in conversation you use these words:

I, I'm, me, and mine. These are our possessive words that the ego connects to who we are and the ego uses them to describe how it wants everyone to see us versus who we truly are (this is our duality).

Your mission? Become aware of how often you reflect to others as your ego (with the use of the four possessive words mentioned). Fill a pocket with paper clips or pennies. Then, be cognizant when you use one of these four words. When you do, take out a paper clip or penny and transfer it over to another pocket. At the days end, count how many times you reflected as your ego to others that day. Now, log this in your journal and write about the experience.

Stillness For Thought:

Value the words you hear and say. It breathes life into them.

Chapter 4

The illusionary world is all around us

Our illusionary world is created by our consciousness. Through what we have been taught, endured, and witnessed.

"Reality is merely an illusion, albeit a very persistent one."–Albert Einstein

Most of us had a very rough ride into existence. Everything was incredible for the first nine months. We had a very comfortable, warm and cozy room to stretch and grow. We were never hungry and when we did have a craving, suddenly it was there for us and we snuggled back to sleep. There was no thought of the past or a future, just the now. Life was wonderful! Until that day when we were introduced to a new womb, a womb with a view! We thought, "Why is this happening to us?" We were pushed, squeezed, and pulled from a warm cozy home into the bright, cold, scary, new, alien environment. And holy crap was it painful! We went through the Play-Doh fun factory and into life. When you enter the world, they turn off the heat, cut off the food supply, and while we're turned upside-down, poked, prodded, stabbed, and suctioned, someone is oohing and making funny cooing noises. What a bad fucking day!

And that's not the worst of it! What has really happened, many never have the chance to discover. We were born into a collective illusion—our life was already created for us. Our world was created out of greed, hatred, and fear with a very small portion of love. These are not the only carriers of responsibility that has molded our world.

Humankind has an inherent destructive tendency, maybe even written in our DNA (as well as the amazing ability to love). It is part of what we are, and it will always be until we discover that one element of stillness and find comfort there. Once we stop reliving the past and seeking happiness only in our future, can we find the wonders that the present moment has to offer.

We as humans love illusions. We pay people to perform them for us. We buy movies, watch reality shows, and play games that engage us as avatars. All these elements draw us into a different reality, an illusionary reality so we can escape our own reality. Not only is this the current state of mind, it has also been a part of us since the beginning of time. In Paleolithic time, Grog was drawing pictures on cave walls, telling stories with his hands, acting out and fantasizing about making that one big kill with his weapon. This could have been the first instance of visual entertainment.

Once language was established, embellished stories were told around the fire pit and served to support the drawings on the walls—how big was that fish now?

Technology has brought us so far now that it's difficult to differentiate between reality and illusion.

To answer the question of why we love illusion so much, I will answer this question with a question of my own. What is easier to believe? Harsh reality, death and mayhem, or a reality buffered with plump and fuzzy kittens?

And what about our first impression of reality? Wasn't the experience of being born, harsh, intrusive and painful? And you may ask how could we even remember this? This is something that the body and mind will always remember, because reality was that painful. This is stored in your unconscious awareness.

Your mind-body connection is there from the beginning and it remembers. So much so, that if you have an easy, in-office procedure like removing a mole, even though the area is numbed, there is still a part of your physiology that recognizes that you're being violated—that you are being damaged, incised. I've witnessed numerous times during a simple medical procedure where surrounding tissue has been numbed with Lidocaine, the patient is awake and talkative—then the first incision is made, and the patient faints even though they feel no pain. The body has an unusual ability to recognize being violated even when the mind is unable to.

If very young children have painful experiences at their pediatrician's office, like mending a broken bone, stitching up a cut, or the invasive procedure of diagnosing a bladder infection, they remember. So much so, that all they need to recall the experience is to see someone wearing scrubs. Their unconscious remembers and children will cry, scream and fight to get away from those bad memories. Maybe this *recall* is an innate ability embedded in our DNA to help us survive so that we can live long enough to propagate the species. Something to think about anyhow.

We love illusion, and we live in illusion because reality is too painful. Then why not just stay in the illusion where everything feels good? Our illusionary life is so seductive, almost erotic in nature at times. The distance between reality and the illusion we lose ourselves in all depends on how we have decided the world needs to look. From the games we play, to the movies we watch, and the books we read, we are moved into a reality created by another that can look and feel fantastic! Even mind-altering drugs have played a role in helping us lose ourselves further in the illusion.

The illusion that we choose can be catastrophically damaging to our mind-body and those we love. The effects are different from one to another. It all depends on how badly someone needs to escape the illusion that they're living. Why didn't I say, "...the *reality* that they're living?" Because it's difficult to determine the causality. Is it the *reality* or is it the *illusion*? Reality-illusion seems to be one real thing.

People who live in a harsh reality and have a taste of—or an illusion of—a grander existence, will find a way to make that illusion their own. For example, people living in oppression-who find a way to escape or leave their country because of the promise that they can live freely elsewhere.

The thought of freedom is a wonderful gift. This is one of the reasons America historically has been sought after and fought over. It's a fresh start away from oppression. There is an extensive legal system that is in a constant flux to make things *fair* (trying does count here). In other countries, there is no word that can be translated into "what is *fair*" for the masses. The oppressed populations of the world make great sacrifices just for the chance to reach the illusion of freedom—to escape reality. Some find it, some don't.

Yes, in America, we do have a grand illusion that we live within. We have the right to vote in this country. If you're over age 18, male or female, drop your ballot in the box and it is counted. And does it count? We would like to believe so.

But, even if your vote is truly counted, at the end of the day, does it really matter?

The presidency seems more like an auction with only one difference between the two candidates—one issue that stands out clearly: pro-life or pro-choice. Where does the money come from that is given to the candidates? It comes from you and me. If you are pro-life or pro-choice, it doesn't really matter.

Wait a moment ... your beliefs do matter to you! And I'm not trying to take that away from you when I say that it doesn't matter. Let me explain. The products you buy, and the money you spend goes to companies as profit. And part of this is given to the candidate that best serves the companies interests. You can be pro-life and the checks you write to support your favorite candidate can be negated by the purchase of products from the companies supporting the pro-choice candidate. The decision is determined by what is in the company's best interest to be profitable. If a large profitable company decides that it would be more profitable for them to support the candidate that is pro-choice, it negates your contribution. So ... put that in your pipe and smoke it. Not a smooth and easy pill to swallow, is it?

If this confuses you or just makes you feel sick with thoughts of "it can't be true," investigate for yourself and discover the difference between what a CEO of a major corporation earns in a year compared to how much our Commander-in-Chief (the President) earns in a year. Big difference!

Our illusionary world moves with and in the direction of the way currency flows. This is a sad thing. The USA doesn't even own the Federal Reserve Bank. This is run by a banking cartel that only a few people know exist.

So, are there people who have lived in illusion and were thrown into reality beyond their control? Yes, you will find them serving when help is needed. I'm talking about the wonderful, selfless people that protect us—our service members that protect our nation, police officers that protect and serve, the EMT and First Responders and everything in-between. These are the people that live daily with the reality of what happens when we're so caught up in our illusion, that we become lost when tragedy strikes. These are the souls that help pick up the pieces and aid us when we're in need of assistance. And these brave men and women do this 365 days out of the year. Even when they're not on duty, it is still within them to act when help is needed. It's just who they are; it is their calling.

So, how do I step out of the illusion that has just been revealed?

Stepping away from our ego and observing the mechanics of it is the first step. Our ego is easily found by simply listening to the voice in your head.

INNER MISSION

What's your mission?

From this day forward I want you to be honest with yourself and with others. Your indiscretion, sins, and regrets are in the process of being released to the universe! So there is no sense in creating any more of these now.

Being honest with yourself about what you like and dislike.

Be direct and honest with others. A yes or no answer is acceptable. Don't feel compelled to provide excuses that are unlikely the real reason for your yes or no anyway.

Those who use "white lies" (even though "white lies" are harmless at times) compromise their own integrity within themselves. When we lie, we create *more* mental noise because we now have to maintain the lie, and this is what we want to steer clear from. Sometimes we tell small white lies to protect us from embarrassment. But who is really protected here? You or your ego?

Once you become honest with your own inner dialog between you and your ego and then with the people around you, you will begin to become free, open and inviting.

Recall the times you have lied. Describe why you lied. Write each reason in your notepad. Tear off the sheet of paper for each indiscretion. Fold it in half and set it on fire, releasing it back into the universe.

Stillness For Thought:

Once you accept and release your past, only then can the present be invited into your life. Remember, your ego is only as powerful as you allow it to be.

Stillness Within the Storm

Chapter 5

Let's go shopping!

In the previous two chapters, I wanted to remind everyone of the nature of humankind. Sometimes this history is lost to us in our daily lives because we're filled with other thoughts and stresses, which doesn't allow us much time for reflection.

Not many of our basic behaviors have changed from the past to the present. It seems that they are innate to our core, more like written into our DNA. We have the ability (and necessity) to follow the same paths of behavior of our ancestors. Granted, we have evolved and learned from some of our mistakes. Let's give us a little credit.

For instance, we no longer blindly send our troops into a hell storm of flying bullets and hope they make it over the hill and to the other side. Learning from our mistakes we now kill more efficiently than years past. Less collateral damage and more focus upon eliminating our intended target. Not to mention, being nowhere near harm's way while doing so. This is one example of what learning from our mistakes and the advancement of technology has given us.

Our innate core behaviors have even been given a Top Ten list of things *not* to do. What *not* to do is still just as prevalent and holds just as true today as it did thousands of years ago. Yet, our bad behavior continues. With little if any progress in correcting what we know and feel is wrong. Sure, we create laws and place checkpoints and stop-gaps to correct our undoing, yet our behavior still continues.

This Top Ten list that I am referring to is the Ten Commandments. If you can grasp the language barrier and the many translations, you can get some basic instructions for "What *not* to do"—a *code of ethics* to guide you.

But, you know what? Even with this guidance, the behavior continues today as it has in the past.

Why is this? What can we do to change this?

If we look closely, we can see that there are issues that we're working hard to solve. But, until our media focuses more on the benefits of living by a code of ethics and less on the negativity of not living by this code, negativity will always overpower our senses.

We've been making an effort on the outer edges and moving into the core of the problem. Will it be enough? I will not give false hope, but there's always hope. Hope in itself, is amazingly powerful.

I honestly don't know if we can reverse all the harm we've caused our shared home in the last 100 years. And there are super smart people working on it. Our earth has an amazing healing ability that we have yet to realize. The only question is: will we be around after the healing has completed?

Let's take a glance at the current state of the world with the focus on "western civilization" and the progress we're making.

On December 20, 2006, with recession looming, G.W. Bush told America to "Go Shopping!"

When taxpayers become unsure and unsettled and in fear—not knowing what to do, throw them a distraction. A new distraction. A new game, or something new to buy. Governments discovered early on that this method works wonderfully.

Not only did it work thousands of years ago, but it still works today. Romans built huge coliseums for this purpose. If the populace were unhappy or unsettled, all the Roman governments had to do is create an event where they threw a few Christians to the Lions to be ripped apart and eaten alive.

The Christians were heathens right? Give people blood, guts, and gore and they seem to forget what currently is bothering them. These Coliseums provided the much-needed entertainment that we craved. They held close to 50,000 people and provided public spectacles of re-enactments, gladiatorial contests, and animal hunts—anything to satisfy our raw ancient hunger that we all crave.

Currently, with technology, we've improved on this simple concept ten thousand fold. Now, all that we crave is at our fingertips in the form of a remote control button. TV, cable, and satellite have entered our lives, our homes—every moment of our existence it seems. Now we always have some type competitive sport year around to engage in. If it's not football, there is hockey, baseball, cricket, soccer, bowling and even fast cars that seem to forever make a left turn around in a circle. We have reality shows where we get to live vicariously through others. We can be voyeurs and watch someone else's daily life on the internet. We have the daily news (local, national, and world) so we can experience the atrocities that humankind can and will commit.

The State Department even spent $250,000 to make a background prop for delivering the wartime daily news to all of us back in Desert Storm. It looked similar to a video game. They showed us specifications of our armament that was being sent out to defend our troops. They used psychological means to make this ongoing war a game to all of us just so the people in power could keep it moving forward!

We have the news on cable how many times a day? At any moment, we can access it in paper form, in the media, and even on our smartphones. All of this is available at our every waking moment from the time we wake up, to our morning drive to work, at work, and on our drive home. It is available to us whenever we desire it. Everything that is on our mind—everything we want to know, is right at our fingertips. But, this comes at a cost—the cost of relinquishing yourself to others.

There are people that want your money. These people have spent billions of dollars to find just what to say, what to present, what visual components to use to make you feel you need to purchase what they are selling. But first, with the use of psychology, they create a "need" for people to want to buy what they are selling. So in essence, the media, psychologists, and the world around us have created our illusionary life. Our wants, needs, and desires are fed to us without us even knowing it. Unknowingly and discreetly, their solutions are fed to us as well to make us feel better.

If you watch the footage of G.W. in his public statement, telling America to go shopping, he says it with conviction. My take on G.W. is that he is just a really simple guy. And when his aides suggest he tell the American public to go shopping in the dark cloud of recession hanging above, you just got to suspect what he was thinking… "Someone is yanking my chain! This will never work! Whose dumbass idea is this?!"

We did receive extra money back on our tax return that year, and we did go shopping and bought things that other people said we needed, regardless of whether or not we really needed them.

Strangely enough, this psychology of creating a buyer started in the mid to late 1920s. It was Sigmund Freud's nephew Edward Bernays who came up with this—one of the first documented methods to use the "human condition" against itself for monitory gain. And the plot thickens …

It seems at the time, the Tobacco companies wanted to generate more profit, and they asked Edward Bernays for help. Men smoked, but there was an untapped market just itching to be tapped—Women. Now the "bad girls" (women of the evening) smoked but not the good girls. So, Edward Bernays glamorized the "bad girls" in advertisements. Then, all the "good girls" wanted to be just as provocative and just as *sexy* as the "bad girls."

I guess that Edward stumbled upon a gold mine as far as advertisement is concerned. Because, "sex sells."

Now prepare yourself, I'm going to scramble your noggin even more in the next chapter when I expose the meaning of life.

INNER MISSION

Your mission? Ask your friends and family: What is the meaning of life to you?

Capture these answers in your journal.

Now, ask yourself: What is the meaning of life? And is it a meaning, or purpose?

Stillness For Thought:

As we move through life and think about it and its meaning, we can passively exist or we can exist in life with purpose.

What happens when we purposely exist in life?

Stillness Within the Storm

Chapter 6

The Meaning of Life

What is the meaning of life?

Have you ever pondered this question? Many have, but how many have answered it? I have the answer for you.

The answer to the ultimate question everyone has sought for ages is just too simple. Everyone overlooks it and most would not agree.

The Meaning of Life is to EXIST. This is universal.

Maybe you don't agree with me, and that's OK. We're not arguing truths or ultimate truths, which can be subjective. Existence is. Seriously, it just is! It's not unlike binary code, where ones and zeros indicate is or is-not. Existence is, or existence is not. Life is, or is not. There may be an in-between, as some would argue, but that's irrelevant to understanding the meaning of life. Since we're made of energy, and energy only changes form from one element to the next (does not cease to exist), we can begin to look at what it means to exist in a similar way. You can see it in our everyday life—nature and the ground that supports the weight of our feet as we transverse across it. In all that we are connected to; the air we breathe, the food that sustains us and the ground what we walk upon.

Is there a meaning beyond, simply "to exist?" If the earth could be considered a sentient being, it would likely be working on a treatment and a cure for the cancer or parasite that resides on its skin. That cancer/parasite is us.

To explore this further, let's break down the meaning of the words we are using.

The use of the word *meaning*, gives us the impression that there is purpose, or there should be. A rock *exists*, and was once a part of the mantel of the earth—it was once a part of the whole. Water *exists* in its compound elements and when you break those apart, energy changes into two parts Hydrogen and one part Oxygen. This indicates that energy changes from one form to another, but doesn't lend anything to a *meaning*. Maybe we should eliminate the word *meaning* altogether.

Here is the reformulated statement on the meaning of life:

There is no meaning to life. Life exists in its own magnificence. It exists in wonder, in its own shape, presence and form.

You may be asking, *"What? Did I hear you correctly?"* Remember, I only said the meaning of life, not *your* meaning—two completely different realizations. I'm describing form in its solidity as opposed to the meaning as you personally see it, which is subjective and meaningful to only you.

We are strange creatures, inquisitive and unrelenting at times. We may be the only ones on this planet that really want to understand and comprehend what is around us, the meaning and the why.

Why do we want to know the meaning of life? Maybe we feel a loss of connectivity to our bond with life. Maybe we want to feel that we have meaning—that there is some magical purpose for us to be where we are at any given time? Maybe there is something within us that tells us that there has to be more. And there is. And you will find it.

When we ask the question *why*, this is because what is *now*, never seems to be enough for us.

We want to give meaning to life because there has to be something more, something better than what we have now—there just has to be! And we play with this idea in our mind, repeatedly. If we just had more money, or if we just had better friends, or if we just had better parents. When we do play with these thoughts in our mind, we create segments of a reality that isn't reality. We give life to an illusion when instead we could've created what we imagined.

We want to give meaning to life because we are told that what we have now isn't good enough—we can do better. And so we focus and strive on becoming better so we can feel we've gained acceptance, sometimes to the point of striving to give meaning to others who we believe reflect who we are. For instance, the proud parent who pushes their child over and over again to achieve what they could never have—so the parent can feel better about themselves and live vicariously through their child. This is just one example.

Others are creating your meaning of life for you. And they have skill and knowledge about how the mind works. Your life is bombarded with sensory overload each day by visual, auditory and sensory perceptions. The main purpose of this book is to help you find your stillness within the storm.

Do we really need a purpose to exist? I don't know ...

There is no reason why we cannot accept life as it is—to marvel in its existence and enjoy its every moment of beauty. It's difficult for us to wrap our mind around this idea of just allowing life to *be*. This is because there are outside influences that don't want you to move in that direction. That would not be profitable for them. A distracted and overactive mind is more susceptible to suggestive influences than one that is fully present.

Although, we do feel a certain pull to find our purpose in life, most of the time, it's simply our ego telling us that we have to discover and accomplish our life's purpose, to make our life complete. Many people have found their purpose in life, so I want to add this disclaimer: *they* didn't find their purpose—*it found them*!

There are many others out there that offer to guide you—to help you find your purpose. But, you know what? Any active search for a purpose in your life is ego driven and soon will be overrun by another purpose. It is an endless cycle.

I hope you can give yourself the chance and opportunity to allow the world to open up to you as you simplify your life. This is what we're working toward. We want to make our life as simple as possible. This allows a busy mind to calm and settle.

Have you ever noticed that when our U.S. presidents get elected they appear commanding and attractive? But after their 4 to 8 years in office, they end their presidency completely shrunken and gray headed? Stress is not good for the body!

Move in the direction of making your life as simple as possible. The meaning of life is merely to *exist*. Inviting a purpose into our life should not be forced. Be patient, and your purpose will ultimately find *you*. And you will feel it within you.

One element to help you begin simplifying your life is: give in to what has transpired in the past—allow it to exist and be just what it is—*the past*.

INNER MISSION

In the next chapter, we will be discussing the past. Joyful and heart-lifting parts of our past we need to hold close to our heart. But, if you are actively participating in "inner missions," you are slowly letting go of your past indiscretion and regrets. Releasing them back into the universe.

We need to begin to let go of elements of the "storm." We can't change the storm, but when we allow the storm to exist, it is easier to accept. Watching world news, national news, or local news, it doesn't really matter, the majority of it is disparaging information focusing on our human elements of darkness. It exists regardless, so why be reminded of it constantly at a press of a button?

Your mission? Break the cycle of influence. Be entertained by watching entertaining media. Be engaged when you watch a documentary on how the human condition is making life better for everyone. Push away any outside influence that "does not" bring you joy. Make a running commentary in your journal of your progress for 21 days.

And yes, you will hear headlines and see them posted in newspapers:

"Wayward, heartbroken youth guns down students, then takes his own life."

Yes, very sad story! There is no need to read any further!!

Say a silent prayer for the ones who were lost. Donate personal time or contribute, to help the family get through the tragedy. But please, please don't read any further. There is no benefit in dwelling on the horrific details.

What if we had two hours a day of popular daily network news that only presented uplifting stories? Think about how this would affect you. Write your reflections in your journal. Also record your daily choices of what you give attention to and how those choices affected you; "death and mayhem" or "fuzzy puppies and kittens frolicking with their families."

Stillness For Thought:

What you focus on expands. Focus on the positive.
~T. Harv Eker

Chapter 7

The past is what it is

All the past is but the beginning of a beginning; all that the human mind has accomplished is but the dream before awaking.

H.G. Wells

The past is what it is and nothing else—although we love to romance the idea that we could play a role in changing the past. And we have the ability to make this illusion a part of our life and get stuck in this repetitive thinking process. No good comes from romancing the illusion of a life we create with, "What if's."

What if I married or didn't marry so-and-so?

What if I had gone to college?

What if I...? This is the creation of fictional situations THAT WILL NEVER HAPPEN! Ground yourself! Picture yourself walking forward and not being able to take a step back. This is the here and now. Get used to the idea. Be here. Be here in the present.

Yesterday is History, Tomorrow is a Mystery, Today is a Gift, that's why it is called the Present.

Oh, how we do forget all those little phrases we've been taught that have real meaning—real guidance. So let's add this as an endeavor to help you create your "Stillness within the Storm." When you stumble across a phrase that you connect with, frame it and put it on your wall in an active area. You could make it a screen saver on your computer—just make it visible for you to see everywhere within your daily life. And here is the reason why …

We are transient beings, and we need to be constantly reminded of what is important to us. If we aren't reminded, we become complacent, and we quickly lose a focus. This pattern exists within us already. We see it in the way we protect pictures of those we love. By keeping photographs in our wallets/pocket books or digitally rendered on our smart phones, we are continuously reminded of the people who are significant to us. We naturally want to remember and share what is most important to us.

But it's easy to get caught up thinking about the past and get trapped there. It takes time and a lot of work to break the cycle of living in the past. There is a formula I can offer as a suggestion to disrupt this vicious cycle. But, it's not easy.

Today, we love to indulge ourselves in dark pleasure. When I say dark, I mean anything that causes negative feelings like fear and anxiety. There is a part of us that feeds off of this dark feeling. There are many explanations for why this is a part of us, and there are many scholars trying to conclude why. But, at this point, we don't need to fully understand this; we only need to accept that there is darkness within us. Accept it and move on.

Visualize this concept: Light equals levity and positive emotions—goodness or good feelings. Dark or darkness harbors negative feelings, emotions, or actions.

You can take this up a level and attach energy and resonance (like a vibration) to both the light and dark, respectively. Some would say that this is one of the Universal Laws that govern our existence. The concept of Universal Laws can be easily researched for yourself—I'm just touching on the

Universal Laws at this point to ease you into the concept and how these laws can influence your existence.

My question for you is: Have we learned from our past undoing? From all the wars and atrocities we have accumulated from the past. I could postulate an answer, and it would be; marginally.

Currently, we're still killing each other over useless, petty nonsense worldwide! This can seem justified by the bigger picture. We are over-harvesting our oceans and interrupting the natural food resupply chain. We are flooding our atmosphere with CO_2 by the use of coal-fired electric generators that keep our economy running and sustain economic growth of the world. Meanwhile, we're draining the last reserves of our oil supply and switching to dirty coal. And the crippled, Fukushima nuclear power plant is continuing to dump radioactive material into the Pacific Ocean years after the disaster. It's hard to fathom the long-term effects.

And again, "Why?"—To sustain the economic growth bubble that we're all comfortable and cozy with.

While I'm not a scientist, it doesn't require too many brain cells to figure out that humankind (the human condition) as we know it will implode within the next hundred years or so. We've outsmarted and unknowingly sabotaged ourselves by overriding nature's ability to create balance. We're cutting down oxygen supplying forests to fulfill our profit-making, over-consuming habitats. Meanwhile, cornfields are squandered—a staple food source in a third world country—recklessly trying to create Bio-fuels. And this results in our increasing inability to feed the poor.

One definition of insanity:

Insanity is doing the same thing over and over and expecting different results.

Does this sound too familiar? If you think about it, we're not so dissimilar to what we were hundreds of years ago.

We still tend to base our life on those who went before us, thinking this-or-that is what was taught, so the best thing to do is follow the example. We do this repeatedly until someone steps out and makes an improvement. We repeat behaviors expecting different results. We push on year after year until an improvement catches on, and others try it and reflect on its outcome. Does this cause a change in thinking? Yes! Is it a positive change? We will only know when the next generation makes another improvement. And the cycle continues. Only our great-grandchildren will see and understand the results.

How do we get out of the loop? Here is the formula to get you started:

Turn off, drop below, and build something new.

It's really quite simple.

Drop below... Live *below* your means. If you focus your life around being told what should make you happy, you have been incorporated into egoticism. Egoticism defined, is a lifestyle of following an economic, social behavior viewed by others as the righteous way to follow and fit in with everyone else. This lifestyle is on its way to becoming a new religion: www.egoticism.com

Building something new... I'm not suggesting that you build a new *you*—I want you to build a new *existence* within this busy world. Let me explain why the goal is *not* to build a new *you*.

Each New Year there is a promise of resolutions. This idea dates back to the Babylonian, Roman, and Middle Ages. The idealism of this concept is focused on self-improvement.

How many of these "New Year" resolutions actually take seed in your life? Lose weight, get healthier, be something or someone different? One reason that you don't follow through on your New Year's resolutions is because they are a creation of your *ego*, and your *ego loves games*, this is how it thrives. Our ego feeds in many ways. As far as resolutions are concerned, it feeds off the attention of others. In the beginning, you are boasting to others that you are making this big change in your life. During said resolution—when work is underway, there is nothing for the ego to feed upon (unless progress is shared in social networks). And when the resolution fails? The ego still feeds off of your self-pity and attention from your friends. It is a win-win situation for the ego. Statistics reveal that only 8 percent of people who make New Year's resolutions, actually reach their goal. Maybe that is why fitness companies pour more money into advertising around the months leading up to a new year—food for thought. So, instead of setting unachievable New Year's resolutions, I'm suggesting an *evolution*.

One of our objectives, maybe our main objective in this evolution, is to simplify our lives. Part of that simplicity will come from no longer allowing our *ego* to drive our lives.

We need to understand that the voice(s) in our heads are our ego(s). The best way to think about this is to think of yourself listening in the background—the one hearing the voices rambling on, is you. The voices are not you. You are the listener.

Sometimes, the simplest answer to any question is right in front of us. And the most difficult part of the equation is getting past the fallacy of what *"should be" (we will explore this more later)*.

The past is, what it is ... *the past*. It has already happened—there is no magic machine that will have any effect on it. But that doesn't stop your ego from trying. If you let your ego run with the thought of reliving the past, there is a good chance that it will. It may even get incorporated and become a part of your present life. A lot of us get stuck in a fictional world we create. Some so much so that it *is* their life. Your ego loves this, because it is its *food for thought*. There's not much of a difference between reliving the past and re-watching one of your favorite shows—both are fictional.

All the past is but the beginning of a beginning; all that the human mind has accomplished is but the dream before awaking.

H.G. Wells

I reiterate this because even *I* still gain new meaning every time I read it. It is *hard* to let go of the past! Give in to the past and allow it to *be*, allow it to exist in its wonderful self-explanation of its own defining. This is the seed that grows a new evolution within you.

I have now started you on a journey. I have presented you with seeds of encouragement and it's currently in *your* hands to nurture and sow.

INNER MISSION

Next we will be discussing "quieting the mind." First, I want you to write down in your journal what this statement means to you. How does "quieting your mind" connect with you and how does it affect your daily life?

Is it "absence of thought?" Does it mean; "being absent" in and of life around you? Is it a "catatonic state" of existence?

Quieting the mind, living in the moment—the now, and being "present," is not what you may think it is. Put simply? Your main focus is not on the internal side of you. The main focus is on witnessing and being aware of everything that is happening around you.

Your mission? Sit stationary for a set amount of time on a park bench or at a central location at any Mall. Then, focus, pay attention to how the people move around you. Your focus is not on you; it is on everyone around you. Listen to conversations. Observe their body language and watch how the people interact with each other. Make notes in your journal of your discoveries.

This will allow you to experience how the "storm" moves around you while you sit focused and still within the "storm."

Stillness For Thought:

>As the minutes and hours tick by, we need to give most of our attention to the moment that is now.

Chapter 8

Quieting the mind

Quieting the mind, mindfulness, stillness within the mind and other related phrases express a desire that has been a part of our culture for thousands of years. So, why do people feel it's important to *quiet the mind* and what does it feel like? How do you do it? This is something for you to discover.

I've mentioned before that we can get so caught up in our *thinking* (the multitude of voices in our heads talking incessantly) that we lose the ability to distinguish between the future, present, and past. This *thinking* can take over our life, and we *become* our thoughts.

"I think therefore I am."

This is a bold statement. And I don't subscribe to the notion of *the ultimate truth* or similar ideas. If I were to tell you that this statement is not the truth, or not a true statement, how would that make you feel? The entity that you are is not created because you think—the entity that you are is based upon biological elements and through the magnificence of life. You are alive! You are breathing! This is as close to magic as we are able to perceive.

A better statement for our evolution is…

I AM!

Anything that follows is just an afterthought.

We have the innate aptitude for *accidental discovery.* You can find this interwoven into our existence as well as within yourself. When accidents happen—good or bad, we learn from them. And those who do actually *learn* from them pass on their genetic material to their offspring. We are curious creatures by nature, and the ones who seek to make their existence easier, safer and more comfortable, seem to live longer and have a better ability to pass on their genes.

Quieting the mind is just one of these accidental discoveries.

Turn the clock back several thousand of years and you will find that we were more in tune with our surroundings than we are today. Partly because today we have so much lit up during the evening hours, that it takes away from our ability to enjoy the dark. Imagine staring up at a night sky full of stars—it has the ability to make you feel really small. It can take your breath away. We've all experienced this sensation at one point or another—we just have to *remember*—think back to what we've experienced. Remember times when we were children. Reminisce about chilly nights when we slept under the stars. Remember nights around the campfire as the hypnotic flames danced and we felt the warmth on our face as well as the hairs we singed while roasting a marshmallow on a stick. Yes, the marshmallow did catch fire, and we got all of the gooey goodness all over our fingers when we made s'mores.

This reflection of a past experience with awareness helps reinforce that stillness is achievable. Since you have unknowingly experienced moments of stillness in the past, you will likely be able to get there again.

Today, if you get away from all the lights around you and in the depth of the evening, you can still be captivated by the night sky. This captivation is the easiest way to describe how the mind can be quieted. This experience of "awe" is written into our DNA.

Quieting the mind

Why don't we connect the dots? The universe has given us a preview of how to *understand* and *experience* what it's like to be present. So, why is the experience of *presence* not integrated into our daily life? I don't know. Maybe the abundance of nighttime artificial light interferes with the connection.

There is one failure in our elegant design; a short attention span. This is part of why it can be so difficult for us to "quiet the mind," because the mind constantly wants to move on to the next thing. We can all identify with the noisy mind that is continuously rambling on. Now, let's relate this to the ego. We've already defined the ego as a noun.

Here is an online definition of *ego*:

A person's sense of self-esteem or self-importance—"a boost to my ego."

A part of the mind that *mediates* between the conscious and the unconscious and is responsible for reality testing and a sense of self.

The rambling in your noggin is this mediation of the ego, the illusion of who you are versus the life you live.

When we quiet the mind or become mindful, we move the subconscious and ultimately the unconscious into consciousness. Shifting in this direction allows focus on one element to complete a task, or to take a test, but it also eventually can allow us to push through the noise and become aware of the "I AM" within us.

Our unconscious acts without thought. You've heard of feats of self-sacrifice or incredible acts of strength to save another from death. When people tell these stories, they tell us that they were "in action" before they even knew it.

The absence of thought is where we create.

Many of us have already experienced *quieting of the mind*—stillness; when we gaze deeply into an open fire or are mesmerized by the heavens at night.

Like me, some of you may need assistance on this journey. On my own path of discovery, to help me understand more about myself, I sought out therapy. This was the best thing I could have done for myself. My therapist listened to all of my ranting and through many months, obtained a good idea of what my story was about.

A book was suggested, which gave me great comfort and addressed the issues I was confronting at the time. One book lead to another and soon I was sharing books with my therapist. I do not claim to be a licensed professional; therefore, I will not give you specific direction to find your way. I will only make suggestions to open your mind to new ideas and point you in the direction of discovery. The rest is up to you, and I highly recommend enlisting the help of those who have the skill set to help personally guide your journey.

My hope in sharing what I've learned is that you will discover which elements inspire—breathe life into you—and draw the people who will guide you to find your unique stillness.

When we seek truth or "reality," what we discover can be subjective, because we're looking for the truth in our illusionary life. Thinking is not a bad thing. The magnificent creation you inhabit supports the ability for your mind to think. But truth is not to be found in the illusion. This is why it is so important to "quiet the mind."

Your ego is alive and still feeding—remember that it doesn't like to be exposed. Within stillness, the ego is exposed. Take moments each day and pay attention to the biological entity that is you. Listen to your heart beat. Feel the air move through your lungs. You are on a long personal journey of discovery of who you really are.

INNER MISSION

Before you read the next chapter, capture in your journal, your thoughts about how important your time is to you. There is more time available to you than you believe.

Time is relevant and subjective at the same time.

Life is really not that short. In our youth, we can't wait to grow up. In our 20s we don't hold the concept of growing up. Our 30s we reflect on our past and wonder what we've done with our life. This is also the time we begin to truly connect with who we are and realize our "years are numbered." 40s? We focus on if we've really accomplished anything in life and where we're headed. Then we get scared.

Your mission? I want you to move beyond yourself and release what you could have done in the past and let go of organizing your future. We can be so focused on creating a comfortable future for ourselves that we neglect the current moment.

Ask yourself these questions and capture your responses in your journal:

Is your primary focus in life on past experiences?

Is your primary focus in life on working for a future experience?

Is this moment important?

Stillness For Thought:

Yesterday is history. Tomorrow is a mystery. Today is a gift. That is why they call it the present.   *–Bill Keane*

Stillness Within the Storm

Chapter 9

Look through me and you will know me

I believe that our hopes, dreams, and beliefs can be shared openly. The idea I am proposing here is: *be open* by being transparent with others in an engaging way. When you are vulnerable in this way, people will find you inviting, honest, and straightforward.

It's unnecessary to blather unchecked with a continuing stream of information that can and will make those around you uncomfortable. Ease into this crazy idea *slowly*. If others start suggesting a mental ward for you, then it's time to back off a bit before you find yourself in a loony bin! Exposing every small detail about yourself in this manner is like taking off all your clothing in the first few minutes of a first date. Yep, no one finds that sexy.

Instead, when it feels right—take off a sock, maybe even your tie! Shed some *mental* clothes when the time is right. It would not be appropriate for you to start peeling away at the layers that created who you are in the middle of your first dinner date.

What I am suggesting is you *can* share openly. There is no need to let it all out at once. Being open to the thoughts of others, listening and commenting without judging, is acceptable *no matter what* social situations you are in.

A great first start is to be totally honest with yourself.

Pull up a comfortable chair and sit with me for a few minutes, and we'll talk a little about being honest with *yourself.*

We all know about white lies and many of us believe they are harmless in nature. We use them to avoid embarrassment, uncomfortable situations, or to delay revealing something we are not ready to share with others (or with ourselves).

There are many reasons why we tell lies. But the question to ask yourself is: why do *you* tell them? Ask yourself **why** as many times as it takes to get the answer.

White lies are not as harmless as they seem to be. What they allow you to do is escape from providing an honest answer, thus pushing aside the confrontational emotion behind the embarrassment, uncomfortable situation, or something that you're not ready to discover within yourself. This becomes habit-forming because it's the easiest way out of the conversation or situation. Or is it?

We tell lies to protect our ego when it really doesn't need to be protected. Sometimes we aren't even aware that we are lying, especially when we are lying to ourselves. Protecting our ego generates many excuses, displacement of facts or even a belief that we are protecting someone else.

Here is an example:

If you are asked to donate money, attend a social event, or approached/confronted on the street for money, a direct "no thank you" will suffice. No more, no less. *Don't give in to explaining the why or why not.* A kind "no thank you" works wonders not only with others, but with you as well. Of course, there will be people who won't take no for an answer. With these persistent people (like someone trying to sell you something), it can take up to three times repeating this phrase before they accept your answer. And yes, it's so much easier to give an excuse—a little white lie to avoid the discomfort of the situation.

For example, how challenging is it to say "no" to children on the sidewalk selling goods to support their activity groups? Very difficult—those pleading eyes, and youthful smiles. If you *need* to say no, perhaps for financial reasons, simply address them with a smile and a "no thank you."

As we continue to get to know our ego, we start to discover the difference between "who we really are" and the role our ego plays in our daily life. The idea of a secondary entity within us quickly becomes not as crazy as it sounds as elements of our ego are exposed and the difference between ego and "who we are" starts to fall into place.

The word "ego" is defined in the dictionary as a noun (and I will repeat this often). Continuing to read, you will discover that there is more to you than your ego. The primary entity within you that most of us ignore, "who you really are," is hidden. This is how your ego wants it. When your ego is exposed, it will become angry. If you want to feel the anger of your ego, have someone explain what your ego looks like to him or her. Some say if you really want to know yourself, let someone who doesn't like you, tell you your faults. If you can hear these comments and walk away with unhurt feelings and a smile—and give an honest and sincere "thank you" to that person—you will be given an amazing gift of insight that few have experienced. Although, I have to warn you about this experiment, what you hear will not necessarily be the truth, but more likely the harsh reality of what *others* see in you—simply a description of your faults as it is reflected in *their* ego.

Think about this for a moment:

What would living without resentment feel like? Who would you become? And how would it affect your life?

When your ego rules your world, the primary entity within you is subservient and passive. When the ego rules *who you really are,* the real you is nothing but a sidekick to your ego—a minion to be controlled. With repetition, your ego tells you who you are and this is who you eventually become. If your ego says that you're ugly, fat, and worthless ... that is who you will become—what you will believe. You will seek others to reinforce this fallacy because it resonates within you. Reinforcement upon reinforcement becomes your reality.

In this way—repetition and reinforcement—subjugating people (others or yourself) is easily accomplished, verbally, visually, and emotionally.

When we are transparent, we will attract authenticity with others and with ourselves. Energy attracts its likeness. The polar opposite of being socially transparent is being socially convoluted. So, would you believe me when I say that we're living in a socially convoluted world? A world where conjecture rules (lawyers love this). And I will go one step further and say others use this conjecture for their own benefit. Our daily news uses words to help us believe something is real when it is only conjecture, in other words, "guesswork."

For example, when the word "alleged" is used in the phrase—"alleged" murderer, we may not pay attention to the word preceding the word "murderer," and decide guilt based on this incomplete perception. In this way, wordsmiths can manipulate what they want you to hear and what they want you to believe. They can rise to great social standing and achieve what is perceived as amazing results up to the point where they are discovered in their deception and ultimately fail. And history repeats itself.

Who are some of the people of high regard and authority who have followed this path? Leaders of countries, states, and many spiritual leaders. Why did they fail, why will they always fail? I'm stepping out on a limb here…

They will fail because they took a well intended message or they took advantage of their position to fulfill their ego-selfish needs.

They have failed because they were trying to be someone who they were not.

Our ego helps us to create a false representation of ourselves and attract the similar energy that is needed to maintain our illusion. This pull of likeness is called: *The Universal Law of Attraction.*

And is defined as follows:

That what is like, attracts the same.

You will come to understand this last statement in time as you read on, and I urge you to do your own research and make your own discoveries. Go to your search engine on your computer and type in; "The law of attraction."

The idea of transparency will be easier to accept when we no longer fear the unknown. Understanding that the past has little value and the future is unwritten is paramount. What matters the most is where we are right now, this very moment. Once you gain the understanding that the past has little value to you and the future is unwritten, the easier it is for you to understand the benefit of living moment to moment, and this experience will open your eyes to all the benefits of what transparency has to offer. The mental folders that constantly attend to and maintain the lies you have told will be gone and so will the guilt.

One of the side effects of transparency is: there is no longer any need to keep secrets. When someone tells you something in confidence, it is just that. But if someone wants to tell you a secret, and you don't want the responsibility of keeping it confidential, you will have the freedom to tell them *"no thank you."*

Transgressions of the past are carried by each of us—you are not alone. They are an invisible weight and necessary nourishment for the ego to feed upon. They hold us down and hold us back—prevent us from doing amazing things. But, once transgressions are allowed to breathe out in the open and are accepted, they dissipate.

The egotic-soup that you have to swim through every day (existing in an ego infected illusion) has a limited attention span. Meaning, there's always something new and fresh for the ego to latch on to and nourish itself with. The ego is distracted easily. We move from one new fresh buzz feed to the next. We are always awash in a fresh new scandal. As we leap frog to the next, the previous is soon forgotten.

Have you ever noticed that when you go shopping for food, you've already made your list, but when you're hungry, items that weren't on your list seem to jump off the shelf and into the shopping cart? Ice cream, chips, animal cookies, little smokies—the strangest items seem to appear.

When you finally pull into the driveway at home, pull your hand out of the bag of chips so you can turn off your vehicle, gather everything up, wander indoors and load everything onto the kitchen counter, your family asks why you brought home 10 cans of sardines! And you don't remember. While the children jump up and down in a frenzy because you bought ice cream, something inside you, thank Edward Bernays, again!

Edward Bernays, an American, specializing in the pioneering of public relations and propaganda, was instrumental in introducing the *egoticism* that we see all around us today: On billboards, on radio, on cable TV and in newspapers—the foundation of every commercial you see today. So, it's not about the 10 cans of sardines that we felt compelled to purchase along with everything else that wasn't on the list. It's about the manipulative application and applied psychology permeating our environment that is driving our urge to buy. Enough said.

Being transparent and living transparently is *first* being honest with yourself. With practice, you'll soon recognize a *feeling* to choose, to be honest, when you could've easily told a lie. There are more persuasive elements circulating around our existence than we could ever think of. Sometimes we *feel* this when we feel that we're being pushed in a direction unknowingly and we don't understand why. It's now time to take a second look at *why* we feel this way and ask questions not only of ourselves, but also of others. Brainwashing is a plausible explanation when our ego runs our life and we're subject and subservient to others. Understanding this helps us to become aware of when we feel uncomfortable, and once we have that awareness, it's time for us to pause a moment and ask *why*. It's time to start being completely *honest* with *ourselves* and not give in to *excuses*. This is the moment where we draw that one line in the sand and feel comfortable saying "no thank you."

Our transparency can be every part of our here and now and accepted by the people we invite into our present. The people you invite into your life will have the ability to enjoy you as you *are* exposed transparently. These are the people that enjoy spending time with you, where there is no pressure and no judgment. When you have no hidden secrets—no hidden agendas, you become a catalyst of freedom in their life. It's an abundance of positive energy that attracts its likeness. If a situation doesn't feel comfortable, there is a good chance that it's not. If someone is bearing gifts that appear free, no gift is free; they all come with a cost. If it's too good to be real, too good to be true—more than likely it is. No thank you.

INNER MISSION

We are about to take on a topic that some people use as a mantra for life, a phrase with the emphasis on how to get the most out of your life.

A lot of us don't take the time to think about this because we are busy doing "something else." Sometimes it takes a catastrophic event like a near death experience or surviving cancer, to *shock* ourselves into taking a second look at our life and what we want out of it.

Your mission? Explore this idea of "what do I want out of life" before it takes a "significant emotional event" to push you in the direction of change. Ask yourself questions about where you are in life.

How content are you with your life as it is, *right now*?

If there were no obstacles, what would you change?

Stillness For Thought:

In the end, will you be angry and demand a second chance; or will you feel content and at peace with yourself?

Chapter 10

Life is short, live it while you can

Life is short, live it while you can. Really? This is a well-known phrase warning us that we better "live" our life because it can pass by quicker than we realize. Or maybe it's more of a realization that we should live quickly before we die. Some even say, "Life is short, hey ... have an affair." I don't know if this last mantra is wise to live by—it certainly could spice up your life and make it more exciting. But, on the flip side it would add much more stress to your life than is advised, not to mention the repercussions of such behavior.

We hear these phrases, and they hit home with a touch of reality. The older you get, the stronger the impact. They make us take a serious look at what we have and what we should've accomplished by now. And yes, some of us have our parents constantly reminding us of this too.

Now, with this warning, comes anxiety as we scramble to fit more "things to accomplish" into our lives. What more can I stuff into my already overwhelming life?

Maybe books on this topic will help, because there is a plethora out there on the subject! But is this really necessary? What are we actually accomplishing by filling our life up with... stuff? Are we getting more "quality time" with our loved ones? I don't think so.

Authors make a lot of money trying to help you find more time in your life. More "QT" (Quality Time). So you read and read to find more ways to squeeze more time out of your day—it has to be there somewhere! Go ahead, schedule quality time along with everything else that you're told is important to fill up your day. Write in everything that you think you need to schedule for your day and write it in your planner. This can make you feel better because now your daily life is planned and scheduled. But, what is controlling you, your *life* or your *schedule*? Now every moment is squeezed out of your life and is mandated by a design of your own doing. But what is the *quality* of the "every last minute" that has been *scheduled*? Something to think about.

Time passes and things come up. Loved ones are disappointed, feelings are hurt, and you try again and again to keep to your planned schedule (insanity). When it doesn't work, you try to plan better.

You could almost speculate that we created ADD-ADHD in our world—because of this mindset. We believe that we have to fill every moment with something to do, or we're not doing something right. We've been taught that sitting with nothing to do is a "waste of time." Again, something that we have created. We don't feel right if we're not continuously stimulated or something is not stimulating our life. We hear it on the radio and see it on TV. Someone is always filling our thoughts with something that they think we should be doing.

We do this planning with our children too. We fill their days with activities: sports, clubs, etc.—things to do to "fill" their days, so they aren't empty. With this, we teach our children that every moment has to be filled with something.

With our society's progression, it is no longer the cultural norm to encourage our children to play outside. And I'm aging myself here … even if it was raining I was told to go play outside! Then again, I had several acres to fill my busy mind with something to do, even though it was raining. I would wander back in when my hands were so cold I could no longer feel them. I'd warm up and get ready for dinner. A lot has changed since then—granted.

We cram and schedule every hour of every day with things to do. We even pass this on to our children, filling up their life with things to do and we feel absent or guilty when there are "gaps" in their schedule.

We believe time is relevant. Most believe it's extremely important. I'm here to tell you, time is irrelevant. Once you start looking into the moment around you and enjoy its stillness, a new world opens up and you realize you can enjoy all the time in the world.

A life without time. When you no longer have to constantly look at a clock to see what time it is. When you wake up in the morning refreshed before the alarm finally goes off. The first time you realize that you can look forward to this new day without dread, and you are encouraged because life is no longer as short as you once thought it was.

When we were young, time was not important. It didn't matter. We had so much fun playing that we would collapse exhausted wherever we were and sleep. When playtime was over and it was naptime, we cried. We had no choice, our complaints rested on overloaded ears. As the door shut, we cried until we had a headache and then drifted off to sleep in our bed. And again, sometimes we would play so hard that we just dropped with exhaustion. When we were young, we had no concept of time—we just lived!

Remember this? We ate, we rested, and we played hard! We lived, learned, lost toys and got new ones. We made new friends and quickly lost the memory of the past. And we always found love in everything around us. Time had no meaning until we learned that we were allowed to do more when we got older. This discovery in itself changed everything!

Once we started to understand the concept of *time* better, time began to move really, really slow. We no longer wanted to be young; we wanted to experience what adults did because they had no bedtime. We wanted to grow up fast!

Ironic isn't it? At one point, time had no meaning, then it went too slowly and ultimately we can't find enough of it!

My one moment of clarity about this topic came to me when I wasn't expecting it. You know what? I never forgot that moment. I was a few months away from my 39th birthday. I was a Medical Assistant working for a premier clinic in adult and family medicine. I started my intake with an elderly gentleman—height, weight, blood pressure and a little light conversation. Out of the blue, he looked at me and said, "Son, please don't wait until you're my age to start enjoying yourself. Because if you do, you'll spend more time attending to your health than you will enjoying your retirement. Go have fun and enjoy yourself now! Don't wait until retirement." I was dumbfounded and speechless by this random statement. I finally responded, "Yes sir."

Another element of understanding I always keep close to me is: *there is as much time as you want to have if you only look.*

In the few years I spent in the medical field, time was a big issue—we couldn't find enough of it. I have the greatest admiration and respect for primary care physicians. Fourteen hour days, 4-5 days a week and Grand Rounds. And they don't make the money you think they do. A new entry-level doctor still has $100K+ student loans to pay off and is making just under that a year. In our clinic, I was brought into a meeting because one of the doctors was always running behind. Normal visits without complications would run 15 minutes, physicals 30 minutes. This doctor was always running 30 minutes behind every day. I raised my hand and presented this suggestion. "Turn the clock back 30 minutes, then the doctor will always be *ahead of time*." I got a lot of confused looks from the clinic administrators and some disapproving nods and comments. Then a doctor within the group raised their hand and explained politely that they already use this idea during the day. But still, the administration thought this was an incomprehensible suggestion. It was just nonsense to them.

I tell you this story so you can employ this idea for your own benefit. If you are someone like me, who is consistently running late, here is a little illusion I use to put myself ahead of schedule. Using our love for illusions for my own advantage, my alarm goes off at 5:30am. I hit the snooze button once. Nine minutes later I turn off the alarm, shower and a half hour later, out the door and headed to work. My alarm is set TWO HOURS AHEAD … shhh, no one needs to know that my bedroom is a time-zone vortex.

Life is short, live it while you can.

Romance this idea: You have all the time in the world, all that you could ever want. We lose and waste a lot of time in thinking about the future (which is not certain) and dwelling in the past (something that already has happened). If you would/could eliminate this thinking (future and the past), how much more time would you have being in the present?

INNER MISSION

We will be talking more about "Your Life" here shortly. What sustains your physical and mental wellbeing—your body and the magic that keeps you alive!

Tobacco products? They need to go! In the U.S., we have a small text "surgeon general warning" on each pack of smokes. In Mexico? In BOLD letters on the front of the carton (not in small text on or below), it states: "Using this product WILL KILL YOU!" Quick and to the point, yes?

Being "stationary" in life will ultimately cause you to be stationary permanently—in the grave. We are meant to be moving and active! Talk with your doctor about what is best for you to be a moving and active participant in your life.

Your mission? Dedicate eight hours of your time for sleep every night. If you are unable to do this, it is time to visit your doctor and have a real discussion on this topic.

Eat healthy food, move your body, plus get a good 8 hours of sleep, every day.

In your journal track your sleep patterns. Log how many hours of sleep you get each night, and how you feel when you awake. (If you don't want to do this manually, there is technology available that will not only track how active you are during the day, but record your sleep patterns as well.)

Stillness For Thought:

Your life is based upon your decisions. Interrupt the noise of others who tell you how you should live, what you should eat and what you should buy. Use the practice of stillness, listen to what your body is telling you. Listen to what your body craves and not what others tell you it should crave. We currently live in excess in the western world. For survival? Our bodies don't need excess to survive.

Chapter 11

Your Life

Let's talk about *your life*.

From the forward of this book until now, we have explored the concepts of who I am, who I was, and who I could be. We have also explored these elements within you. Who you are, who you were, and what you are capable of. Our goal? To contemplate, discover and learn; to reflect upon how we have changed and progressed throughout the existence of humankind, and how much we have changed on a personal level within our lifetime.

Can we really say humankind has changed deep down inside? Can we say that we've progressed and learned from our own negative past behaviors and have made changes to correct them? And have we become more compassionate, more caring over the few thousand years of documented history? Or are we still stagnant and unchanged? Have we regressed in this new age we live in, or have we progressed in the ability to be good earthly citizens? And a more important question to ask: Has the progress of technology moved us in the right direction? Technology has almost doubled our life span. Yes. But, is this a good thing?

The jury is still out on that question.

Technology has allowed us to kill more efficiently and allowed us to select our targets better and harm fewer innocents in the wake of war. Killing is never a good thing. In the balance of eliminating those who cause greater harm, is it better for the greater good? Here is another thought: There is so much hate and disparity in this world, does it seem like we are becoming more evil or less evil?

Technology has granted us the gift of recording life in real time. This allows the viewer to be right there at the moment when something happens. It's the ability to share something wonderful, something funny, or something dreadful. And it can be instantly shared with all points of the globe. Has this made us better humans? Has it made humanity more caring, global citizens?

The jury is still out on that question.

The difference of the perceived evil in our existence between a thousand years ago and now is just a matter of the type of recording and the amount of footage from those able to record the events.

Today, it is hard to escape the news. It is everywhere! It is on the computer, in the car, on your flat screen, in the newspaper, on billboards as you drive to work, and just an arm's length away on your smartphone.

A few thousand years ago, you had one village scholar "Orian the volumetric" ringing a bell, bellowing his message as he walked through town. You had "Jobe the teacher," writing down stories to share. And let's not forget the community crazy person "Lepts, the insane," babbling incoherent messages and screaming at others as he wandered down the middle of the street.

Is humankind so much different than they were a thousand years ago? Has there been a shift in how we treat each other?

The jury is still out on that question.

Let's segue to who we are and who we believe ourselves to be.

From the beginning of this book until now, we have been exploring the elements of who I am, who I was, and who I could be. And we are still exploring those elements within you right now. We have contemplated our past in who we were, who we are, and what we are capable of. This may be the only good reason to look into the past.

We have the opportunity to reflect upon how we've changed and progressed throughout the existence of humankind. And again, how much we've changed on a personal level within our lifetime and to what extent.

We tend to reach far and wide to capture that one understanding—that *one* element that makes us. *Who are we and how do we fit into all that is around us?* We endlessly search for these answers within nature, old writings, and digging deep within ourselves. In this search, we tend to ignore where we currently are. We ignore the ground right beneath our feet. It seems that we always gravitate back to that influx of two different states—the past and the future. I say this because we're always looking outward to solve the puzzles that confound us instead of looking inward to resolve the issues from the inside out.

Currently in our world community, we are looking outward to space to solve our problems, to colonize a new planet, a fresh start. Planning excursions to create a new world to call our own... or is it just to exploit the new resources? (I think the latter description is the most prevalent.) All the while, we ignore the ground right under our feet! Instead of healing our world, we are quick to abandon it. The open wound that has been left by industry, pollution, and corporate greed is not being treated. It is being neglected. The unfortunate result of forward progress is our destructive evolution.

We (our global community) are currently "paying for" the inability of the powerful people at the time to "take heed"—to be forewarned. This mindset is as prevalent today as it was long ago.

This is the world that gave birth to us, gave us life and sustains our livelihood. Yet we can easily overlook and forsake mother earth for another untouched world that we can further exploit. My own personal view is this aspect and pattern of behavior is predictable for all sentient life that grows in this universe. Maybe that is why we haven't discovered life out there in the beyond that is readily available and easy to reach.

Maybe it is because the people before us progressed to a technological point and just withered under their own weight. Like a fire that burns hot, burns twice as fast.

Maybe intelligence has already come into existence in the universe. Burned bright for a short few thousand years, then faded into extinction. It seems that we are the same. Over the course of humankind, we have lived a smoldering existence before we turned industrial. Right now we are burning brightly, hot as if we were on fire. We are over extending our resources to sustain our existence. Our life upon this world is not even a nanosecond in universe's time, maybe so insignificant that it is immeasurable as time is measured.

In our egoticism, we burn through resources and discard what we no longer need. This idea is infectious and it spreads like a wildfire, like an uncontrolled evasive parasite that feeds until there is no more to feed upon and then dies.

At the very base of this egoticism is the life we have created for ourselves. And so far, what we haven't discussed is the *life* that is *you*. We've touched on this topic a bit in previous chapters, so let us just dive in.

The life entity that is you and all the biological functions between your body and brain sustains the life that is you. The autonomic functions between your brain and body regulates itself.

You don't have to tell your body to breathe, digest food, excrete waste, or even encourage your heart to pump blood. The body-brain works in the background, hidden from your thoughts to sustain your life autonomously. This is an independent relay between your brain and the functions of your body.

Here is the most significant part: The body-brain works in harmony within this autonomic system, in harmony with each other to sustain your existence. A support structure so that you *can* fulfill the meaning of life. Existence.

Life is being, life is existence, life ... is.

Now, let's not confuse *your life* with *life*. They are two separate ideas. They are different, yet connected and intertwined. The gift that you are, supports the life exterior you have created for yourself.

Here is the defining difference: *your life* has been created by you. Your parents created the *life* that is you by engaging in sex. And I am sure they had some influence in helping you create *your life* by personally interacting with you... from the way they behave to how they view the world. Your parents' influences created the foundation for you to construct *your life*. And *your life* as an adult is basically an accumulation of your own personal choices that grew from the foundation your parents gave you.

Your life, which you created, and its foundation *can be* witnessed as an illusion. Remember I said *can be*. The illusion of what we perceive of every element that is around us sustains the illusion of who we are perceived to be. Here is an example:

You can be told over and over again by the people that are around you that you are unattractive, ugly, with no possibility of any type of future with anyone. If enough people say this to you over a period of time, it becomes reality. But it's not real; it is an illusion created by someone being unkind. It was you who gave meaning to the idea to make it become true in your illusionary world. Your consciousness resides in the illusion that is *your life*. Your unconscious knows that this illusion isn't true.

We can entrap ourselves in the same way by letting our ego chat away in our head, telling us the same type of things. "This will never work," "I'm so pathetic and unlovable," "I'm so miserable"... Attach any negative feeling to your thoughts about yourself and what happens? You resonate negative emotions, and those around you pick up on this. They see it in your body language; they feel it in your energy. This leads to what some people call a "self-fulfilling prophesy."

You can see this happening with children who follow in their parents' footsteps. And they are such comfortable shoes to fit into because we cannot be faulted if we're just like our parents. We can't fault our children if they behave the way we have. And our parents cannot fault their own behavior. The behavior bar was set to this height. Being stationary and level with it is acceptable, but children rising above their station are every parent's dream. We also have parents who live vicariously through their child's life by making the child overachieve where they've failed.

Your life is a collection of experiences guided by social norms, shaped by your environment, which creates the illusion that is *your life*. What does this mean? It means that your ego runs *your life*, not you.

Our parents are responsible for giving us life. Genetic traits are bestowed upon us from our genetic lineage. Environmental social conditions can enhance or degrade our behavior by forcing choices to be made. For example, growing up in a loving and happy environment will suppress the gene that fuels aggression. Whereas, growing up in a violent and depressive environment awakens the gene that helps you survive both physically and mentally at all costs even if it's beyond the law. Basically? We all come from a family heritage of survivors. It is bred into us.

What we choose to do with this pool of genes that each of us harbors is up to us, it is up to *you*!

We are all a sum of our collective experiences from birth to now. And since our gene pool has been passed down from generation to generation, all that collective innate ability has been passed down to us too.

We over-analyze even the smallest details at times. We regurgitate the past and speculate about the future, even debate them both. But, to what end? Some ends of this regurgitation have a means—to encourage new understanding.

Our technology has progressed to a point where it can predict our behavior and predict the quantitative outcomes. These predictions are an educated guess based on watching people move in a certain direction when they are confronted with something new. It is similar to trapping a rodent. You study its behavior, watch how it lives, eats and breeds. Then you change its environment, set traps and see how it behaves given the new conditions.

Companies study their customers in the same manner—only trapping them into spending more money.

This means, in order for companies to be more profitable, they have to become really good at developing algorithms based on our human behavior to influence and alter our wants, needs, and desires. Then, use this information to direct our behavior where it profits them most.

There are those who analyze our behavior so they may postulate and dictate the profitable corporate earning future. In turn, they do this so they can sell this information to those who would profit from it. This is a big vicious money-earning circle.

The past is unchangeable. This is one of the most concrete observable constants. It is unmoving and inflexible. Yet, we like to *fantasize* about changing the past and are often unconscious of its unchangeable nature. And still in our mindset, we play at fictionally viewing our past as if we can change elements of it and the possible outcomes. If we could have a better understanding of the past and change what has transpired, what would it solve? And there is no need to solve it because it already has happened. Just accept it at face value and move on. Stop thinking about it now and let the past exist as it is. Let it go. ***Once you accept and release your past, only then can the present be invited into your life.***

Most of us are currently swimming in the influence of others' wants and desires, which are directing our lives. Take control of your life by eliminating the noise around you.

The cable companies are struggling to keep customers. Not only are many of us finding ways to "skip" commercial advertising, but, many of us are have discovered that it is much less expensive to get our entertainment from companies that provide it without commercials. Because of the lack of revenue from this method of advertising, companies have begun paying to have their product featured in TV programs and movies, rather than creating a commercial which may never be viewed. In the next show you watch, you just might see the characters drinking sponsored beverages, wearing designer underwear and clothes, and driving sponsored cars, while verbalizing endorsements for the product brand.

In the next chapter, I will further define the difference between the biological element that is you and the egotic illusion that has created what you call *life* based strictly upon your ego. This will help you to understand more about how your ego fits in with everyone else around you.

INNER MISSION

Do we ever take the time to stop and think; where are we in our evolutionary stage of development in our existence? No, I guess that not many of us do.

Politics and religion have not changed much over many hundreds and hundreds of years. Both are still are driven by the need to perpetuate the myth to further an agenda.

But science, unlike religion and politics, continues to move forward and evolve, unafraid of change. Scientific methodology is shaking up the other two communities, making many people in those communities nervous and uncomfortable. Both politicians and religious entities are scrambling to hold their ground. But, people are losing faith not only in politics but religion as well, which could lead to changes in the evolution of our human condition.

Your Mission? Discover the depths of your belief systems. Science regularly recalculates its measurements. So too, should we take the time to reevaluate what we think we believe.

Explore the boundaries of what you believe.

Ask yourself, "What do I believe?" In your journal write down whatever comes to mind. Then ask yourself, "Why do I believe this?" Continue to do this for each belief you hold as true.

Stillness For Thought:

If truth is subjective, isn't the illusion of reality subjective also?

What we have left is: faith in what we believe to be true.

Stillness Within the Storm

Chapter 12

The Human Condition

"Any intelligent fool can make things bigger, more complex and more violent. It takes a touch of genius—and a lot of courage—to move in the opposite direction."

- Albert Einstein

In my research, I find myself constantly drifting to quotes of Einstein. Albert Einstein was well read and understood by most as being a magnificent man that changed the world we live in. And as I share his quotes, I hope that it will lend some continuity to all that you are reading here.

Einstein is still an enigma to many people. People were so captivated and intrigued by his intelligence, that Einstein requested cremation upon death to prevent tampering with his body. Some people worked behind closed doors, without permission, to remove his brain, and cremated his body without it. His brain was then suspended in a jar of solution, to study it. This was all in an attempt to understand how he was capable of making such astounding discoveries. Did this violate his last wishes? Yes. Has it helped us to understand his intelligence? No.

The discoveries that Einstein made were based upon work completed by others in his field. He did not make all of them on his own.

He didn't invent. He gathered, accumulated, used, and referenced ideas from people before him (some known, some not known very well… I am speculating here). And with this information, he was able to link theories together that we are just *now* proving to be important not only to our life, but the universe that is around us.

Humans are builders of not only structures, but of ideas and concepts. Some of the structure and art of an ancient past still exist today such as temples, statues, pyramids and paintings. Some of the earliest paintings are still on cave walls. Artists are inspired not only by nature, but by the complex structure of how nature creates itself. Anyone who creates builds on concepts that they visualize and are inspired to "add in" their own perception of what they are seeing. They are building upon existing ideas. When we look up into the sky, whether it be night or day, we find images. We can draw connections between the stars to create new images. We watch clouds form into recognizable images. This is our yearning to create.

Paintings can inspire artists to create different images from what they see within other's art. Similarly, architects create structures influenced by other buildings or other art. It's not so difficult to understand how scientists are influenced by other scientist's work and how they take that inspiration and move forward with conclusions of their own.

Today, we are advancing so rapidly in our scientific, mathematical, and technological evolution that new discoveries are difficult to keep up with. Scientists have said that if we stopped all of our advancements now, it would take 200 years to incorporate and assimilate all of what we have learned.

Dreamers constitute an openness to change within the human condition. They gravitate to and attract each other. Like moths to light, they seem to gather and exchange ideas. And when they share their dreams with others, ideas build upon each other. There are some people who have written stories to share with others about their fantasies.

Science fiction has been a driving force in realizing the technology that was previously fantasized about. Science fiction writers of the early 1900's were influenced by one amazing inventor's ideas on what the future would be like. This same inventor gave us the electrical current to supply our world today, and he gave us Alternating Current or "AC." The progressive, futuristic production (all electric) vehicle was named after him: Nicola Tesla, or just Tesla. This same inventor created the Niagara Falls generating plant along with Mr. Westinghouse's financial support.

There are so many wonderful people who've contributed to the life we live today. And sometimes we take this for granted. Our great, great, grandfathers would tell stories of their childhood: "In my day, we would walk to school, even if a blizzard was storming!" "We had to walk 10 miles uphill in a blinding snowstorm at times." "Well I'll tell you what; we had to walk 10 miles, uphill just to get home from school."

And when we got home?

We had chores to do. "We had to thaw out the cows just so we'd have milk for the morning breakfast." "We had no fancy breakfast boxed cereal to eat in my day… We would steal grain from our stock animals, crush it with a hammer and pour frozen milk on top! That's what was for breakfast! And we loved every bit of it!!"

We owe a lot of our current existence to the dreamers of our past. And sometimes we forget about them and we take what we have now, the world around us… for granted. With little thought of who helped bring us here.

Today, we have cell phones so advanced that we are connected with everyone and everything that is important to us. If we have a question, press a button and ask. Our phones even alert us when a child is lost or taken from their home. The speed of technological advancements is staggering.

The learning curve to use our new technology is becoming so simple and intuitive that wristwatches are obsolete, while some Amish still use sundials. We are moments away from getting an answer to almost any question we ask.

What time is it? Look at your smartphone. What is the weather like outside? Look at your smartphone. How are my friends today? Look at your smartphone. Our access to information and our social networks is so quick that it helps us feel confident and reassures us that almost anything we want is within reach! Oh, and my prediction? Our phones in the future will be more like our best friends, carrying on dialogs with us during each day. They will wake us up with a warm greeting in the morning. They will verbally warn us of our surroundings. Tell us what to eat and what not to eat. Maybe, even suggest we attend to our children and significant other.

The point that I am trying to get across here is that we have a propensity, a need, and desire to improve everything around us. Meaning, there is still hope for us in our human condition. We are idealists!

Here's a not so new idea: *Laziness is the master of invention.*

We want to get the most out of the least amount of action. Why drag something when you can roll it? Why roll it when you can pull it? Why pull it when you can teach an animal to do it for you? Why walk when you can ride? Why ride when you can have a trained animal pull you on a cart with wheels? When we figured out that animals require a lot of work to care for we created steam, electric, and the internal combustion engine to power our conveyances.

We are builders, we are dreamers, and we are creators! We are killers, we are destroyers and we are dissemblers. We are lovers, and we are haters. We have the capacity for much love and compassion, yet we have the propensity for much hatred and demise. And yet we still thrive and exist within the current human condition.

So, how did Albert Einstein accomplish all that he did? I have a theory. My theory is this: Einstein was so amazed with the mathematical thoughts in his mind that every waking thought he had always gravitated to the visions in his mind, calculation upon calculation, forever building equations upon equations, formulas upon formulas, and theorizing where no one theorized before. He was excited, and his excitement continued to build with every new theory that fell into place. He attracted the universe to him—this is the law of attraction, otherwise known as "The Secret."

When we allow the world to move through us, it controls us. We are within its destiny, its control. When we make the world move around us, we receive what we ask of it and influence the final outcome.

Einstein stumbled upon this "secret" and gave up his past, and thoughts of the future. Nothing else mattered. He was so focused on the now, he allowed the world to move around him.

He theorized... every waking moment. And when he didn't have enough time to do so, he created it. He was so excited about his equations that the element of time found him. When we become excited about an idea, we can become consumed by it. We are the human element that builds and creates.

Understanding the human condition reassures us that we are not much different from others that lived many years ago... the main difference is that we have time to learn from and build upon the ideas of those before us.

I have talked about how "egotic" we can be, and gave you an idea of how we are currently moving through our egoticism. More or less, it is our daily routine.

Our ego is a cornerstone of our human condition. How it feeds and how it is fed has a direct influence on the direction we take as individuals.

We can start by taking ourselves out of our routine by opening our world to understanding more and demanding less.

Open up your mind to the wonderful working elements of everything around you. Feel the earth under your feet as you walk. Listen to your own heartbeat. Feel the touch of the wind upon your face. Stop and let the world around you fill your senses.

We all live in a world that is bigger than our single self. In some way, shape, or form we are not only connected with each other as individuals, we can also be seen as connected as a whole. This is why we are not yet extinct. We have the ability to share so many elements of our human condition with each other without even knowing it. Each of us shares our intention, our feelings, and our current path or direction every day—the moment we address the first person we greet in the morning. Our "mood" at the start of every day will change the people we address in our morning routine. It can't be hidden from others, although it can be shared. Your mood is always shared openly and without thought. Your emotions resonate to those around you. There is no hiding it.

Understanding more and expecting less out of life brings you closer to allowing the storm around you to move freely.

Allowing the storm to move around you is not a passive state. It is an *active* state of awareness and understanding. Just as you sat still and allowed the people to move around you in the mall as an exercise… listening, watching and learning. This is the active state of stillness. It is the quieting of the ego to allow the world around you to exist and move in the way it is going to move. As the human condition will move it to be so.

Sometimes it is really hard to let go and allow the human condition to simply exist as it is. We feel that we can fix it. But this is not what it requires. It only asks for your help. Start by making another's day brighter. Your actions contribute to positive elements of the universe.

Buy some lemonade at a youth's lemonade stand. Personally thank a Veteran for protecting your freedom. Drop a quarter (or several) on the ground for others to find. Leave a big tip for someone who has gone out of their way to make your meal just right. Donate your time so others will receive value from it. Providing change in someone's day can be as simple as a greeting and a warm smile.

Our human condition is what it is. You can't take much away from it or add any more to it without changing who we are. The next chapter we will discover how to live in our own world, yet share personal experience with those around us.

INNER MISSION

Allowing the storm to move around you is not a passive state. It is an active state of awareness and understanding. Just as you sat still and allowed the people to move around you in the mall as an exercise… listening, watching and learning. This is the active state of stillness. It is the quieting of the ego to allow the world around you to exist and move in the way it is going to move.

Sometimes it is difficult to let go and allow the human condition to exist as it is. We feel the need to fix it. But it doesn't need fixing, or could we fix it if we tried.

Your mission? Begin to look at your *expectations*, of yourself and others. Do you *expect* the people in your life (including yourself) to behave in a particular way, to say or do specific things? How attached are you to those expectations? How upset do you get when things don't go the way you believe they *should*?

What are your expectations? Write in your journal three things you expect from someone else, and then answer these questions:

Do they know you expect this? What is the worst that can happen if they don't meet your expectation? What would happen if you let go of this expectation completely?

Stillness For Thought:

How do you let go of attachment to things [or people]? Don't even try. Effort creates attachment. Attachment to things [or people] drops away by itself when you [your ego] no longer seek to find [validate] yourself in them.

–Eckhart Tolle

Chapter 13

Shared Box Theory

The idea "understanding more and expecting less" is a new foundation to help you on your path to finding your stillness.

Day to day life for most of us is a no-brainer. Seldom do we contemplate how all of us, together in this world, weave the fabric of our existence. I desperately wanted to come up with an easy concept that would motivate us to pause and think a little more about this idea. That is when I came up with an idea of "Shared Box Theory." I hope to model how each of us interact (knowingly and unknowingly) in our day-to-day life.

I've studied the blending and overlapping filters through which we all see our world. Yes, we all see things differently through our own perceived life filters or lenses. We all have to ability to understand at times that we are all different, and we can see things differently. Push your filters aside and let's get into a *box*!

About the same time as when my fiancé and I were preparing to move, my long lost twin sister and I were reunited after many years of separation. She and her daughter offered to help us pack up and move (and then unpack). My fiancée Julie, my twin Lisa and her daughter Aly, our son Chase, and I accomplished this task in one complete day.

I realized that our life (my fiancée and I) and all of our junk from the past seven years of living together was being exposed openly for others to see, feel, touch, and experience. Our life was being shared openly with others—although not in the expressive manner such as an invitation, but as a necessity to move stuff from one point of residence to another.

Our stuff—things that others normally don't see like collections of movies, trinkets that hold sentimental value and well... just odd stuff—was on display for all to see. Reflecting on our move, I realized that we capture our memories, thoughts, feelings, and experiences (good or bad) and collect them like keepsakes. We box them up and store them, not only physically, but also *mentally*! Based on each experience, we choose a storage method (physical and mental): opened, easily opened, guarded, shared, lost, chained up and hidden, or even buried. If you really want to know someone, go through a box of their stuff. Or just volunteer to help your friends move.

This helped me realize that we wander through our daily life, presenting a box that is opened to what we want others to see. We all do this. This is the human condition. And when we come in contact with each other, our boxes overlap, bump, or crash into each other. The elements that we jointly share match like puzzle pieces, and we connect with our shared box elements or our life experiences.

With this thought, our guarded "boxes" play an inaudible note of their own. When they are disturbed, they tend to *sing* silently in their own harmony. These boxes have their own resonance and play their own tune that cannot be hidden—a note that can be known by those who we share "boxes" with—unknowingly.

We guard our real beliefs and thoughts to avoid the scariness of being vulnerable to fear of rejection. This is an element of our human condition.

But our true thoughts and intentions will always find their way to the surface. Sometimes in ways we don't intend. Like a "Freudian" slip (an unconscious wish to express an intention), we accidentally say what we really feel. Our notes that resonate within the very atoms that create us, express the intent of who we really—our past and present. Understanding the law of attraction can help you understand this resonance more.

At a glance, others see what we want them to see—our appearance; the clothes we wear, and the way we present ourselves, packaged for others to judge—as well as our age, gender, race, height, and weight. With one glance, we have the ability to automatically categorize who we see in front of us. When we get closer to someone—interact and converse with them—our "boxes" overlap and find matching puzzle pieces which click into place based on commonalities between us.

Puzzle pieces connect from the collision and overlapping of our boxes. Sometimes we aren't even aware that it is happening or don't understand why it is happening, but simply feel a gravitational pull to another.

Imagine an existence where individuals, with their unique boxes, are moving into and overlapping with others. When all of our boxes overlap, no matter who we are or where we are, we can find some shared element that we can understand universally. This is the life that we share.

Given this concept of moving boxes, which overlap with other boxes, are there others that happen to be moving in the same general direction? Our direction? It is natural for us to share our common experiences. The more aligned our experiences and harmonics are, the more we feel "connected" or "attracted" to overlapping boxes that we come into contact with.

INNER MISSION

When we say that another person "hurt" us, because of something they said about us, what does that really mean? Can words really "hurt" us? Words have no physical substance. Words are *symbols* used to describe our perception of the world around us and allow us to express how we feel. How does a symbol, go from being simply a symbol to being the source of pain for ourselves and others? And who is responsible for the "hurt" that is caused when this happens?

The message accepted, is solely dependent upon the receiver.

And yes, this may be a little unnerving. What you hear and accept is *yours* to own. I say this because you do have a choice. You have the choice to take the words that are spoken as credible or not credible, plausible or not plausible and then decide, does it matter to you?

The choice we make often perpetuates our illusionary life. It is up to us to decide for ourselves. Ask yourself, "Do I allow people to control how I feel by the words they say, or do I dismiss their verbiage and accept that what they say, is for *them to own—their* opinion?"

Your Mission?

In the next 21 days, you will no longer take responsibility for, or accept others criticism without examination. If someone is pointing a finger at you, remember that there are three fingers pointing back at them. In your journal write about the times you've released another's criticism (by not accepting it as truth without scrutiny), because it was theirs to own.

Stillness For Thought:

Why do we give others so much credit for making us happy? Why do we feel so good when we point out the failings of others? Why do we try so hard to be liked by others?

Why not simply *be*? *Be yourself* for the sake of being who you are. Be compassionate when others fail. And hold those special people who love you unconditionally, even closer.

Stillness Within the Storm

Chapter 14

Of Sticks and Stones

In this challenge of life as we know it, we often forget the basics that we were taught as children. The basic phrases of nursery rhymes engineered to help us remember parts of the past that have long since been forgotten.

"Sticks and stones may break my bones, but words will never harm me."

This is a simplistic and elegant nursery rhyme designed to teach us when we were young that words in themselves are just that... *words*.

Let's look at this phrase from a tangible and intangible perspective.

The *tangible* would be something you can physically touch; by contact between your physical skin and the object. You can say a word and imagine everything behind it. You can feel it, and yet it is *intangible*. The intangible such as thoughts and words hold little substance, but they can feel like tangible items. Try this, hold something tangible in one hand and imagine holding an intangible word of the same value in the other. For example, hold a stick in one hand, and imagine holding the world "pain" in the other hand. Which object weighs more?

In our illusion both can seem to weigh the same, and sometimes the word seems to weigh more than the object. In the egotic world we live in, words do weigh more than physical objects, which is part of our egoticism and human condition.

Everything becomes clearer once you make the distinction and decision to separate the tangible from the intangible. From what is simply talk to what is solid and something you can physically touch.

Sticks and stones may break my bones, but words will never harm me.

"Words can never harm us." Stick and stones can harm us physically, but words can destroy our ego (which is our illusion of who we are, not who we truly are).

Let's explore, ego as a *noun*.

Nouns can be concrete nouns or abstract. Concrete nouns are tangible. Abstract nouns are ideas and concepts—you can't experience them with your five senses.

The amazing element of biological magic and existence that you are is a concrete noun. Your ego, on the other hand, is an abstract noun of fuzzy ideas and concepts. This is why we can reference the ego as the *illusion* because it is abstract.

Here is a question: Why do we feel defensive when someone uses the word "ego" when referring to us? Obviously, it is not because they are referencing the biological element that we are—they are referencing something abstract, something we can't see, taste, hear, touch, or smell.

When someone exposes your ego, how do you feel?

There is a dramatic difference between who you are and your ego. It is the duality of yourself that we talked about in chapter 3.

"Sticks and stones may break my bones, but words will never harm me."

How we can incorporate this nursery rhyme into our daily life?

The message is sound advice, the significance of the concept is life changing, and the rhyme is ageless. Then why is it so difficult to incorporate this one simple rhyme into our daily life? What prevents us from living life without taking to heart a comment that may or may not have been directed at us? Words are not solid, not tangible. Words can describe what "sticks and stones" are, but words can't poke us with a stick or hit us with a stone. It is up to each of us to make the distinction between the tangible and intangible.

Words are words. They don't become real until we allow them to influence what we believe. Do you have an ego that can be damaged? No. Because your ego is an illusion. Can an action caused by a sharp object cause damage? Absolutely. Physical damage is an observational constant, whereas words are a projection or intention of thought.

The following phrase is an example of the intangible, the written word, becoming tangible, through the actions taken based on its message:

"The pen is mightier than the sword."

While the sword can change a few people from being alive to being dead, the pen, with all of its potential for creating inspiration, can facilitate epic change when it is in the hands of a skilled wordsmith. When a charismatic speaker communicates those penned words, the world changes.

The pen is mightier than the sword.

And so, my fellow Americans: ask not what your country can do for you—ask what you can do for your country. John F. Kennedy's Inaugural Address, January 20, 1961.

Recognizing the tangible and intangible can be a challenge. In our Egoticism, there is no difference between the two. The intangible threat can cause as much or even more pain than physical harm because emotions are involved. Learn to separate the two and you will soon discover that the significance of *intangible* events more within your control than you may have originally believed.

INNER MISSION

Give yourself permission to look into the past—to the specific times when you thought you would never get beyond, that a situation was impossible to overcome. Give yourself permission to remember how it felt… the fear, the anxiety and the hopelessness—the anguish. Remember how overwhelming it was at that time.

Now, here is what's important… You are here now—alive, functioning and reading this book. All of those impossible situations that you came across in the past… you have OVERCOME! Meaning? You have succeeded in working through the problems that were presented to you. And throughout our life, it seems that we have a consistent record of working through problems that are presented to us. It is part of the human condition. If we have worked through so many difficult times in the past, why do we automatically expect the worst from our current situation?

Things happen and you learn to deal with them.

Your mission?

Document every time you've felt like the world around you was collapsing in around you, and write stories about how you conquered or moved beyond every situation. And how you grew as a person because of this circumstance.

Stillness For Thought:

When the adversity of life, presents a chaotic event and you feel like you are falling apart or unable to deal with it, how do you deal with it?

As children, we learned how to cope with problems based on those circumstances in our childhood. Are we still responding in ways we learned as children, which are no longer relevant in our lives? What prevents us from actively confronting people or situations and causes us to give in to the will of someone else?

What is the driving force in your life that directs your choices?

When you are given "lemons" in life, do you "make lemonade?"

Stillness Within the Storm

Chapter 15

This Too Shall Pass

"This Too Shall Pass."

This is an eloquent phrase alluding to the impermanence of everything, an understanding of the transcendence from one moment to another. Here is a commonly told story of an unhappy king looking for happiness to help illustrate the meaning of this phrase.

There was a king who was very unhappy with his life. He had prosperity: gold that he could run through his fingers and bountiful lands of grain, and fruit. He had the company his harem of women, all standing in waiting. Yet he was still unhappy.

He had everything. All he had to do was make a request, and it was his, whatever he wanted. Yet, he found some element in his life lacking.

The answer to his unhappiness came to him in a dream. So, he sent his council out into his kingdom to seek the one thing that would make him happy. As fate would have it, his answer was delivered, but not in the way that he expected. Magistrate after magistrate brought different spices, extracts, and oils for him to try, in order to elevate his happiness. None worked; there was no lasting happiness.

But, one magistrate brought something he didn't have— an ancient sage from the far reaches of his kingdom.

This wise sage stepped forward.

"My king, your magistrates told me of your unhappiness. I can only offer you the gift of this ring to help ease your unhappiness."

The ring had an inscription written on the exterior:

This too shall pass.

"I'm sorry, my king. I have no wealth. This is the only gift I can offer you to ease your pain and unhappiness," he said. "When you are feeling lost, hopeless, or melancholy and nothing else in the world seems to help, please look at the ring on your hand and remember this one important message:

Each moment is not permanent. Remember that all of the obstacles, dilemmas and issues you have ever experienced are now in the past. When you are challenged with unhappiness, look to your ring for help. It will remind thee of past challenges that were overcome. The past seems insignificant now and although it was earthshaking at the time, now it is not so noteworthy."

This Too Shall Pass.

As the king wore the ring, it frequently caught his attention and reminded him of the wisdom of the sage and the written words. And he began to understand. What was revealed to him was that everything he owned and possessed had made him happy for a short time, then the feeling went away. Then he remembered elements from his past that seemed so traumatic at the time but had not truly been that important.

"This gift has provided me with wisdom," he thought as he looked down at his ring. "What I possess or could possess will be lost, taken from me, or leave me in some way. Tomorrow's day is not written until it happens. And I find myself not feeling elated, but content with what I see, feel and experience around me... now."

What really excites me is that there are timeless messages in stories, and parables found in our culture. Passed on for generations, and still, the message has the same meaning now as it did then.

Within the egotic element we currently live in, within the western world, what many of us hold closest is sparkly, flashy expensive objects that make us feel bigger, better, and more important than others. Huge, expensive houses, big shiny cars and trucks, and personal products that make us look better than someone else. This is our newest religion, this is our Egoticism. And like the story of the king, we need some element to constantly remind us to be grounded—a message to continually remind us of what our chosen values are. It needs to be visual so it will stick and create a habit within us.

Others have incorporated this concept into the art around them in messages that they see from the time they wake up to the time they climb into bed. Just like those commercial jingles that we can't seem to get out of our heads, repetition helps etch the message in our memory. Create a personal message to remind you of what is most important to you. Make it visible in whatever manner that you choose and place it where you will see it every day.

There are many of us that already do this without even knowing it—those of us who wear a gold cross, a symbol of the Buddha, or even an image of a loved-one around their neck. They are accomplishing the same thing I am suggesting: a visual representation that is close by and reminds them on a personal, even an intimate level, what is important to them.

Personally, when my world tries to turn me upside down, I only have to look to my left forearm for guidance. Inked (tattooed) on my arm is a message that reminds me every single moment of what I hold true when I start feeling lost. What is most important for me to remember and provides the guidance I choose:

This Too Shall Pass.

INNER MISSION

In the human condition, we acknowledge that there are threats around us. Whether they are predatory, environmental or even acts of God (This is a legal term used to explain happening outside human influence). Threats have always been around but now we are living in the age of "Threat Management."

Large corporate institutions are taking this seriously. Seriously enough that if you display anger or rage in any way, use "R" rated language around others, you get a trip to Human Resources. If you damage anything while doing this, even if it is your own property, you are walked out by security. If you call the police for a domestic disturbance, one of you is going to be taken out in handcuffs.

Rage and displayed anger is your ego unleashed without restraint. This is what the new *threat management* is attempting to control.

Your mission? Identify what triggers anger within your ego. Make a list of the triggers and write them down in your journal. Think of things you can do to remove the trigger points. Be creative. For example, if a pet is the focus of your "trigger," maybe it's time to find them a new home. If crying of your young child is a trigger, maybe earplugs will take off the edge and allow you to deal with the situation more efficiently.

Stillness For Thought:

Find peace within yourself and you will find peace in the world around you.

Chapter 16

Of Light and Dark

Anything that perpetuates darkness pulls you further from the light. Light illuminates darkness.

When you are continually pressed upon by darkness, the lumens of light are diminished.

I will explain more on this and how it affects you discovering your own *Stillness with in the Storm*.

I was in the YMCA one day, music blasting, my legs and arms pumping away on the elliptical. Some reality show was on one of the TV's in the distance. The sound was off, and I was too far away to read the closed captions. But, the message of the show was so terrifying that it jumped out at me even though I was far away.

They had abuse survivors as guests on the show reliving the horrors they had endured. The audience was openly weeping, fully engaged and enthralled in this dark tale. It was almost like they shared the same pain. It was all there: fear, hopelessness, and emotional and physical pain. Everyone was captivated by the story, hanging on every single word, anxious for the story to continue. The show seemed to do a fantastic job of manipulating the audience to tears. We can all fall victim to this psychological manipulation. There are people that want you to return to the show after the commercials get done persuading you about what to buy next. The primary purpose of this reality, prime-time, cable network show was to put money in the pockets of others at the expensive of your emotions and earnings as well as at the expense of the "abuse survivors." These types of reality shows should be avoided. They are just emotive candy for the mind.

Negative energy should not be underestimated. It seems darkness is easier for us to adjust to …Turn out the lights in an empty room and we fall into darkness. Turn the lights back on and it takes more time to adjust to the brightness. Darkness is easier on the eyes. Light takes more time to adjust to.

You could say that negative energy appeals to all of us in a variety of ways. It is easy to give in to it, to be swept away or caught up in the moment. Suddenly, all rational thought is thrown out the window, and you get pulled in. The irrational negative energy takes hold and flows through you.

You've seen this in videos captured of rioters. Regardless of the reason the riot began, heated anger is exposed and released. Bystanders get caught up in the actions of others because of the abundance of anger (dark energy-*darkness*) which is sustained and which spreads to others who then unleash their *own* pent up anger. It is a snowball effect that law enforcement works hard to prevent.

I am guessing that hand-to-hand combat in the Dark Ages was fought with similar zeal. Understand that darkness is a part of who we are. We are all capable of acting based on the darkest parts of ourselves.

Anything that perpetuates darkness pulls you further from the light. Light illuminates darkness. When you are continually pressed upon with darkness, the lumens of light are diminished.

You can begin to understand how we can be attracted to circumstances presented in a group atmosphere. We have all experienced this feeling of connection, whether it was at a concert, listening to a powerful speaker, or even watching a reality show. When we pour our thoughts, feelings, and emotions into action, whether or not it gains momentum, of good or bad intent—doesn't matter. The moment has been given life. It will exist as long as there are those who keep the thought alive and give it strength.

Anything that perpetuates darkness pulls you further from the light. Light illuminates darkness. When you are continually pressed upon with darkness, the lumens of light are diminished.

Here's an example of a situation that we can all relate to, that may help you better understand this concept... Imagine there is someone we have been forced to be in close contact with for an extended period of time that never, ever has anything good to say about anyone or anything. You can feel the influence. You can feel the vacuum drawing you closer and closer to their madness. This is a type of darkness, the unconditional pessimistic attitude. This behavior is contagious and can stick to you like glue. In the beginning, you may believe you can help them, but if you spend enough time with this person, you will become like them.

Crazy is what crazy says and does.

Life's challenges make it easy to become upset and angry. Ask yourself this question: Why is it easier to think of something that will make me angry and put me in a dark mood than to think of something that brings the light of joy to me?

Try this little experiment: Go to a "dollar store" and buy two pairs of googly-eyed funny plastic glasses. You know the ones, big red eyeballs on springs that wobble out and spring back and forth. The next time you get into an argument with someone, put a pair on and offer the second pair to the other person. Continue the argument and see what happens.

What happens? Something amazing that you have to experience yourself. We hold so closely, so innately the inflections of our facial features to recognize emotion that the funny aspect of false cartoon eyeballs, springing out of glasses on your face, renderers the argument powerless. The argument no longer exists. The "argue" has been removed from the "meant." Anger cannot exist when levity or comic relief are presented.

For whatever reason, it is easier to fall into the darkness than it is to climb out of it. We all feel fantastic when the sun is shining down upon us, and we feel the warmth against our skin as our body absorbs the much-needed vitamin D. We shed our clothes to soak up more of the warm goodness. Love affects us in like ways.

The sun does not always shine just as love can sometimes be elusive. We know and understand that the darkness of night is always just hours away, but we have to force ourselves to remember that the light precedes darkness—an unending cycle.

Love penetrates darkness and gets its strength from light.

Next, I will help you understand how this plays a vital role not only in your daily life, but your health also. And how a stressful life can ultimately impact your health.

INNER MISSION

I'm sure you've already thumbed your way to the back of the book and noticed that there are no references listed to backup my theories.

The human condition is made up of builders, creators, disassemblers, thinkers and investigators.

When we focus upon disproving a theory, it takes away from any valuable content of the message being offered. I encourage you, the reader, to resist the temptation to flip that internal switch of debate, the switch that wants to categorize what is right and what is wrong. Although I do understand it will happen.

Investigate what draws your interest and build your *own* theories upon them.

Your mission? Highlight in this book, everything that grabs your attention. Is there a theory of your own developing? Write your thoughts in your journal.

Stillness For Thought:

If bold, intelligent people, in our history, didn't rebel against their dogma (if they didn't fight the oppression of their time and risk their life doing so), we would not have the ability to express independent thoughts openly, now.

Stillness Within the Storm

Chapter 17

The Designer Disorder of the Day

Your ego can play a vital role in your health and how your body maintains itself.

I can clearly remember, years ago, when I was caught up in my own Egoticism. My plate was full, balancing my needs and my family's needs. I remember I often had the feeling that I was in pain even though I had been prescribed three different medications to help me through this rough point in my life. I took two similar medications in the antidepressant category and one to settle my nerves. These pills were a "band-aid" placed over the festering wound that I was becoming. Each person deals with stress differently.

Have you noticed that there seems to be a rising number of "disorders" and "syndromes" that people are being diagnosed with? The conditions seem to grow steadily as time progresses. We have disorders of the mind; we have syndromes of attention and of the digestive system. Why are there so many and why do the problems appear to be on the rise?

Disorders of the body, for instance, autoimmune disorders, can be the direct result of what's going on in your thoughts about your past and present life. *Our ego has the ability to intensify our emotional state and elevate it to a point where it interferes with our physiology.*

Your body is prepared to react to any situation instantly and automatically (also know as "fight or flight") fight, flee, or freeze. This is a natural defensive response when you are faced with a life-threatening situation. When your mind is in a hyper-arousal state, your body reacts by dumping loads of adrenaline into your system in order to deal with the situation at hand. Along with adrenaline, cortisol is also released, which is a natural steroid hormone that your body produces. It is produced in the zona fasciculata in the adrenal cortex. Its response is to increase blood sugar (which also suppresses the immune system) to provide the needed energy to react to the current hyper situation that is presenting itself.

Reliving a memory(s) of the past can also trigger this same hyper-arousal or an acute stress response. Your body feels the stress response and reacts by releasing adrenaline into your system regardless of whether the threat is real or imagined. The autonomic system is not wired to decipher the difference between the real or imagined threat. And sometimes all it takes is something that reminds us of a past threat to evoke emotions that cause our body to respond as if it's a real threat.

Your body is not designed to live with a constant flow of adrenaline in your system. And over time, your body will start breaking down. This is when you will see autoimmune disorders that can only be treated and not cured.

Occam's razor is a problem-solving principle devised by William of Ockham (c. 1287–1347), who was an English Franciscan friar and scholastic philosopher and theologian. His principle states, "that among competing hypotheses that predict equally well, the one with the fewest assumptions should be selected." In other words the simplest available theory need not be the most accurate (if it looks like a *fish*, swims like a *fish*, smells *like* a fish, tastes like a *fish*, it just might very well be a fish).

When the mind is locked into unresolved issues that it can't or won't resolve, you can experience the physical effects: anxiety, inattention, and sleepless nights where your mind is on overdrive and keeps buzzing with thoughts.

Since autoimmune disorders have not been discovered in DNA in a way where a treatment or a cure can be developed, I am going to look to Occam's razor theory for the root cause and possible cure. The simplest available theory may be the best available theory.

If you are over 40-years-old, when you were a child did anyone mention an autoimmune disorder? When was the first time you learned about the existence of this disorder? There are now over eighty different types of autoimmune disorders, and their root cause is still a medical mystery.

Let's travel back in time to the 1950s, the era when the "Happy Housewife" was created.

There were advertisements of wives greeting their husbands, taking care of the kids, and keeping a tidy house. Everyone was *happy*. There were articles written on how to make life happy for your husband; how to act, how to make him feel, how to present a clean home, and how to be a "good" wife.

Women are more inclined to visit the doctor than men when they feel something is wrong. That is one of the reasons why women on average outlive men by eight years. They went to their doctor and explained their problems to them. This was a thriving time in the medical field of discovery and doctors had new medications to treat afflictions in pill form. Women would visit the doctor and the doctor would hear their symptoms of depression, weight gain, a woeful life, and... Guess what? The doctors prescribed amphetamines to them. No wonder they were happy, skinny, and always on the move. Amphetamines create a euphoric state of mind.

The effects of amphetamines on your body is like watching your favorite movie on an old black and white TV set, then watching your favorite movie on a new eighty-inch High Definition flat screen.

Yes, it is that much of a difference. Please don't get me wrong. I'm not promoting the use of drugs, just attempting to paint a picture of the effect the use of these drugs had on their user. Mental alertness was enhanced along with the ability to stay focused and awake longer. This hyperactivity also engaged the body's metabolism to burn more calories. For the doctors at the time, it was the perfect cure. Also, the medical field soon discovered that the light that burns more brightly, burns more quickly.

Now, back to Occam's razor ...

Two-thirds of those diagnosed with an autoimmune disorder are women and this disorder first showed up in the 60s. One of the new medications that were introduced in the 60s was birth control.

Keep in mind, I'm not a medical professional, I am simply providing an educated guess based on my personal observations.

I think the origins of this disorder is a combination of the constant stress of our industrial modern life, the body releasing too much adrenaline for an extended period of time, and too much processed food with toxic additives.

The pressure and complexity of surviving in today's world, in our Egoticism, seems to have taken a major toll on our health and well-being.

What seems real can be an illusion. We are caught in a state that is somewhere in the midst of reality, of what is not real, and of what others tell you is real. So in today's world, why is the media promoting messages on an hourly basis to question us about feeling depressed? I believe there is a corporate entity behind this messaging that realizes that there can be a big profit—a goldmine—selling the idea of happiness, in pill form.

INNER MISSION

We are just one pill away from happiness, or so we've been told by the advertisements in commercials and infomercials.

Pharmaceutical companies promote selective serotonin re-uptake inhibitors or SSRI's. These drugs *inhibit* your naturally produced serotonin from being reabsorbed back into the brain. Changing the balance of serotonin can help the brain cells both send and receive chemical messages, thereby improving mood.

Other drugs like opiates stimulate the production of serotonin and release them immediately, and with regular use inhibit the natural release of serotonin until the drug is taken again. Eventually, the natural process of serotonin production in your body will return once the pill is no longer being taken. But quitting these drugs can be problematic; to say the least or catastrophic.

Our ego is like one of these drugs, thriving on our suffering. If we get well, we no longer need either one of them (the drugs or our ego). And like a big corporation, looking to make a fortune, our ego, will stop at nothing to have us continue to see ourselves as sick and helpless.

Your mission? Discover and document your thoughts about what causes depression. Do you believe your thoughts can affect your health and well-being? If so, what thoughts do you have now that are affecting your life today in a negative way? What new thoughts could you create to affect your life in a positive way?

Stillness For Thought:

Positive thoughts, generate *positive* feelings and attract *positive* life experiences.

Chapter 18
Antidepressants

Before I go any further, you must be asking yourself, why am I switching gears to talk about antidepressants and what does it have to do with me reading this book?

This is for the people who feel trapped, empty or have lost hope in their current life. The reason for this chapter is to help you understand there may be a difference between what you have been told is the onset of depression and the clinical diagnosis. And this is the honest conversation you and your doctor may need to have.

Clinical depression is a serious disease and not to be taken lightly. If you currently are on antidepressants or antipsychotics in any form, you need to follow what your doctor, psychiatrist, or therapist tells you to do no matter what meaning you formulate from these writings.

Have these discussions with your provider and therapist on all your thoughts and feeling—be completely open and honest with them. They will give you hope and guide you in the right direction.

Antidepressants are understudied, but their purpose and function seems helpful for short-term use.

I've seen good short-term results with the use of antidepressants. But, if the medication is taken long-term without talk therapy, its use can be counterproductive. They can do more harm than good in the long run. This is my personal opinion based on my own observations.

If you are currently using one of these drugs, I would like to suggest a new approach to your prescription:

Take your medication as prescribed but in conjunction with bi-weekly visits with a Psychiatrist, Physiologist, or Counselor. Ask both parties to contribute to a joint decision on the continuing use of the prescribed medication. *Don't* take them without counsel or talk therapy!

If I could re-write the rules for prescribing antidepressants, it would be as follows:

Antidepressants will only be prescribed under a cooperative effort between the provider and therapist. The renewal of prescribed medications will be dependent upon follow-up visits to the provider and biweekly visits to their therapist. It will be a joint provider/therapist decision to continue, discontinue, or alter treatment that may be available.

It's important to work through the cause of the depression, rather than only treating the symptoms. It's also important to have a professional help determine when it's time to discontinue the treatment.

And your recovery from depression can take time. Give yourself the time you need.

Elements of our life need to be given time to progress and evolve. They need to be allowed to take shape and form naturally in their own time. When we forcefully mold elements of our life into the shape we think they should be, this can lead to unforeseen consequences that we could have never imagined.

Is depression the new "buzz" word today?

Media sources are promoting ads for depression, almost on an hourly basis. One possible reason for this is the billions that can be pocketed by the makers of anti-depressants. I read a short article years back in a small medical release, which stated that a scientist had found a cure for the common cold. I thought to myself, this would be a fantastic move forward in medicine. Finally, a cure for the common cold. I thought to myself ... this idea would be squashed like a bug! And sure enough, I haven't heard anything else about it in six years. The cure for the common cold and the potential revenue from the "cure," dwarfed in comparison to the billions of dollars of revenue providing only temporary relief of symptoms. The common cold is a serious moneymaker. It's sad, nevertheless accurate.

How can you be sure that you are being prescribed the appropriate medication for your condition? Definite questions to ask, not only your doctor, but also your pharmacist.

The underlying element of depression is "sadness." We are not born into this world with sadness. We are not born depressed. Depression is something that develops over time that begins with sadness.

Depression is primarily an ailment of our thoughts. It's often an outcome from the fear-based illusion of our ego rather than anything to do with our biology.

Depression doesn't happen overnight. It takes weeks, months, years or decades to progress from *sadness* to the state of *depression*. Therefore, we need to be patient with our recovery and *not* expect or seek out a "quick fix."

Our current culture... the Egoticism we live within, promotes the message, seek *quick* cures. We have a fast life, and fast food to help us deal with the fast life. And now we look to the medical profession to provide *fast* treatments to whatever ails us. But, when the warning label on a medication that you're being prescribed mentions, "Thoughts of suicide should be reported immediately to your doctor," you should probably take the time to weigh the benefits versus the side effects before agreeing to the prescription.

Feeling sad is part of our human condition. When sadness is left unattended, it can lead to depression.

When you feel sad, don't ignore it, don't leave it unattended. Acknowledge it, allow it to be, and then shift your focus to the things and people who you feel happy around. When we recall our most treasured memories we can completely shift the way we feel: the first smiles of our children, their first giggle, the comfort of time spent with friends we love, or the joy of falling asleep with your soulmate, fingers interlocked.

The riches of existence are simple. Welcome those people into your life who treasure you as you treasure them.

INNER MISSION

When we say, "You make me," followed by a word that expresses emotion (happy, angry, sad, etc.) we are giving control of our emotions to someone else. We are making them responsible for how we feel.

When we take back the control of our emotions, take responsibility for how we feel; rather than say, "You make me happy," we say, "I feel happy when I am with you." There is no causality here. You are expressing solely how you feel, without tying those feelings to the other person's behavior.

Typically, if we start a sentence with "You …" we are probably either trying to gain control (impose our will) over another, or give up control (subjugate our will) to another. Both of these options are ego driven and detrimental to our health and well-being.

One way to experiment with this, when possible, is to begin your sentences with "I" rather than "You."

Your mission? Observe when you use "You" statements instead of "I" statements, then, in your journal, rewrite the statements using "I" instead of "You."

Example: "You always throw your socks on the floor."
Rewrite: "I feel frustrated when there are socks on the floor. Because I feel like I have to be the one to pick them up."

Stillness For Thought:

We are most embarrassed, angry and upset when our secretive ego is exposed and out in the open and displayed for everyone to see.

Chapter 19

You make me feel

Are we a victim of the world around us? Do people in our life *make* us feel better or worse?

You make me feel.

My first introduction to this concept happened when I was about 11-years-old. I was sad and crying about something I had done that my dad criticized. When he discovered that his words had made me cry, he said, "Did I *hurt* your feelings?"

All I could do was nod up and down and sniffle … At that moment, I understood that I had emotions that were called "feelings." These were mine. In that same moment I realized that I could be damaged by other people's critical comments, and was not responsible for my own emotions. My emotions were completely dependent on others around me. In other words, I would always seek to please others to gain their approval.

This is a lesson most of us learned at some point in our childhood, and we are now going to embark on the journey of undoing that learning.

Other people don't *make you feel, you choose* what *you* feel.

Many of us put the highest value on what others think and feel about who we are.

Think of how this statement affects you ...

"You make me feel ...

Many of us use this phrase often in our lives because it gives us an "out." We say, in many ways, "It's not my fault." We believe, "I am not to blame because someone else said or did it, not me. And now I feel sad and want to tell others what was said or done to hurt me."

This is how our egotic system works.

I am not who I should be because someone else failed to help me become who I should be.

It's someone else's fault.

You make me feel ...

When you say, *"you make me feel,"* **you are handing over the control to another person to determine your happiness.**

Replace this phrase with, *"I feel (this emotion), when..."* Most of us are not familiar with expressing our feelings this way, so it may take some time to get the hang of it. Feel the difference between when you declare, "You make me feel..." and "I feel *(this emotion)* when ..." It is the difference between you relying on someone else for your happiness and choosing, and owning your happiness.

Once we take responsibility for how we feel, we can begin addressing the issues that we have within ourselves. This is a stepping-stone to taking responsibility and taking back the parts of yourself that you have freely given to others.

This sets in motion the ***movement of the storm around you*** not through you.

Never give control to others that allows them to tell you how you should feel. This is one of the reasons why I ask you, to stop watching commercial advertisements on cable TV. We need to own our thoughts and feelings. To take time to dig deep and investigate within ourselves. We need to fight off the feeling that someone else can control our thoughts and feelings. Our thoughts and feelings are ours to own and understand.

Imagine your life experiences as a selection of TV programs. "Confidence is your "remote control." With the TV remote in hand, you control the channels you want to watch (choose the life experiences) while the others around you get to sit back and watch what you have chosen.

Granted not everyone will like your choice of channels. But, those who sit next to you and break out the popcorn and offer you some… **keep those people close.**

INNER MISSION

The reason why it is hard for us to accept reality is because we are focused on what has happened in the past and what could possibly happen in the future. We often don't take into account where we are presently. Maybe because the present is boring and nothing is happening right now; and our mind wanders to a time in the past where something was happening, or to a time in the future where something possibly could happen, bouncing back and forth, until something terrible happens that drags us back to the here and now.

A significant life-changing event can cause us to confront our own mortality and reevaluate what is important.

When this happens, suddenly the past and the future have no meaning. The only thing that matters is now.

Your mission? Reflect on the life changing events that have occurred in your own life. Write in your journal about how these events have molded your life and shaped who you are today.

Stillness For Thought:

Simple acts of kindness are one way to help us be *present*.

- A warm smile when a passerby makes eye contact.
- Saying "thank you" when someone compliments you.
- Saying "no thank you" without "excuses."
- Holding a door open for *anyone* who needs it.

Chapter 20

It is, what it is

It is difficult for us to accept the things around us as they are. We feel the need to control our circumstances. We want to label, dissect and force our own ideas upon everything and everyone. This takes us away from our present self and thrusts us into the illusionary world.

In our human infancy, thousands of years ago, we existed within our environment as a symbiotic partner or "one with nature," hunter/gatherers, living off what the earth had to offer.

Curiosity has evolved us from being symbiotic and existing cooperatively with nature, to being parasitic, even creator (god) like. Many refer to this as the "human condition."

This progression from living off the land to bending our environment to our wishes has happened rapidly. We've cut down the rainforest to create more grazing land for cattle and homes for the prosperous. The rainforest converts toxic carbon dioxide into oxygen and releases it back into the air, which provides the air we *breathe*, to *live*. But it can be difficult to see the "big picture" when you are tiny in its shadow.

When we believe something should be different than the way it is, I call this the fallacy of *shoulds*. A faulty reasoning based on your perception that something *should* be different than it currently is—your community may also justify your rationale. This false perception contributes to our suffering.

Within our own personal *stillness*, resides a nice cozy place where there are no thoughts playing fictional stories of our alternative past life (what could've been, what should've been or what I would do differently if I had the chance). We can *guide* our future (not obsess it) by paying attention to what we would like or where we would like to go. Our stillness resides within that "sweet spot" of understanding that we lived the past, learned from it, and are *here now*.

Here is the secret to creating your own stillness:

In order to set the universe in motion to create and grant our *stillness* to us, we must first form a vision of what we would like our future to be. This is a pleasant state of mind in its creation. Visualize yourself in that moment of where you want to be. Be specific on its creation and the detail within it. Make yourself the center of it. Think to yourself, "this is exactly where I need to be at this moment. My world is not a measurement of time, only a series of moments as one transcends to the next." Focus your thoughts on the element of satisfaction when you are in your *stillness*. In time, this will come to you easily and you will begin to connect with possibilities and situations that will seem to drop right into your lap. Feel the connection and move to the next moment.

In our lives, there are no coincidences. Opportunities are all around us—waiting for us to engage with them. In our Egoticism, we are blind to them because our mind is awash with subliminal messaging and illusions of our creation.

If we look at life and events that unfold around us and refer to these events as happening beyond our control, then we better be ready to accept them as they are. When we finally understand that our life exists within the "human condition as it is," we can rest at ease knowing that this is the natural state of what we are.

When we become possessive with events around us, we take a personal judgmental approach to life as events unfold. We become a controlling element rather than a passive one.

Another way the ego feeds is when it passes judgment on others and compares itself to its own justified identity based upon the strictest, most righteous views of society.

Then our ego soars: "I am good, and you are not. **You are bad!**"

The human condition *"is what it is."* We need not become consumed by what should be right and what should be wrong—there are some who live their entire life in this conscious thinking. If you want to make an impact in life because you feel something is out of balance, purposefully move in the direction of that goal, but understand it's probably not going to happen overnight. Sometimes what is most important to you can take years to find you and sometimes it strikes you like a lightning bolt.

Where we are right now is a struggle for power between your conscious and subconscious state--your conscious being the ego (which represents who you currently are in your illusion) and who you really are that is arising from your subconscious. Once you make that transition, you will know it! When I crossed that threshold between the conscious and subconscious, I was lost... I didn't know who I was anymore. Believe me, this is a good thing.

INNER MISSION

If you think part of the world around you is unjust, create momentum within yourself to take an active role to correct the injustice.

If sadness consumes you when you see homeless people, identify what you can do to help. Move from thought to action. The action you take doesn't need to be grandiose; it just needs to be *action*.

You are beginning to uncover *who you are* without ego, this is a challenge. Give yourself time. It will come to you.

Your mission? Start mapping out what is important to you. Fill your journal with written notes and ideas. On this list of *what is important to you*, think about the activities involved and how you will begin to engage with them.

Plan an event or activity.

Do participate and review how it went.

Act upon what fits and drop what doesn't.

If something doesn't fit? Try something else.

Stillness For Thought:

If you are *still* and listen closely enough, there is no need to search for your calling, your purpose in life. Because, it is already there, right in front of you.

Chapter 21

Start defining what is important to you

We have two distinct parts of ourselves, separated yet connected.

In our Egoticism, money, power, and fame are what attract others to us on a surface level. The money we have, the home we live in, and the car we drive determine our place in this ego-based system. But there is more to each of us than our image; more than we can possibly imagine.

Where Egoticism has lead us is to valuing people with accumulated wealth as superior to those who support the daily existence of others. This is how Wall Street works. Unless we shift this thinking, and unless the world shifts to valuing humanity as more important than materialism, we are lost and our human existence may end in less than 100 years.

Moving our collective existence forward, sustaining life and everything we are is the utmost challenge being presented to humankind and the human condition. If the world were to unite, we just might extend life another 100 years. There may need to be a catalyst—something that we can all rally for—some significant element that tells all of us; if we don't do this, we all cease to exist.

When we look back millions of years and ask how mammals survived in spite of the catastrophic extinction of life on our earth—we recognize that life is resilient. Life exists to exist. This is the meaning of life. Our purpose in life can be negotiated.

We all currently reside in the Egoticism that is presented to us. The choice is up to us. We must ask ourselves, "What is most important to me? How do I want to be remembered?"

Egoticism does not appreciate people who fall away from its ego-based system. We live in Egoticism because it is easier and more comfortable than taking on the transgressions that reside within us. We are creatures of taking the easy, most pleasurable path.

Our duality presents "forks in the road" to choose which aspect of our being we wish to operate from; Living in our conscious life or allowing our subconscious to ascend to the surface. In other words, in each moment we get to choose either: to continue forward in our egotistic life and bathe ourselves in Egoticism; or choose to push beyond ego and allow our true voice within to respond to our life.

Remember, the material things that you acquire in life are just that, things you have collected. They are objects. Maybe they have some sentimental value, but they are still just trinkets. They can be lost, sold or squandered. The memories of the shared life experiences—no one can take these away.

As the end of your life, what will you value most? Will you feel accomplished because others are jealous of the wealth and flashy things that you have accumulated (which, by the way, you can't take with you)? Or will you feel accomplished because you chose a life of personal substance over material substance? When you choose the freedom of the latter, rather than the prison of the former, not only will you dig deep within yourself to create balance within you personally, but also the changes you make within yourself will overflow to others.

Your freedom inspires change in the people around you.

Start defining what is important to you

If you feel that the world needs changing, the change begins with you.

Every time you put something positive into the universe, the world changes. Your kindness invites miracles to show up. Not just in your world, but in the whole world. –Author Unknown

INNER MISSION

Next chapter we will be disclosing how your ego sustains itself. This will be easy! No, I lied...

Your mission? Create three fictional stories about yourself, providing background, a beginning, middle, and end. One is a sad story, one is happy and one is crazy. Make the first two plausible and the crazy one seem like you are clinically insane. Write these stories in your journal, then read them out loud and comment on how each story makes you feel, during and after reading them.

This mission can cause an over-feeding of your ego, and help you to discover where your unconscious will finally start pushing your ego aside.

Stillness For Thought:

Your ego wants you to believe that you must constantly strive to be better than others. But, when you are your authentic self, you have no competition.

Chapter 22

Is it diet time for your Ego?

It's time for our ego to lose some weight.

Feeling defensive is the primary indicator that our ego is in control. When we feel defensive, our ego is in self-preservation mode—it doesn't want to be exposed. Being exposed could lead to its death or non-existence. And, make no mistake; it does have a reason to be afraid.

Our ego wants to feel "right" and important, "better than" others. It feeds on *validation* from others and demands to be recognized—to be known: "Recognize ME! I am HERE and I will not go **unnoticed**."

What happens when our ego screams for attention and doesn't receive it? Just something to think about.

We need to place our ego on a strict diet.

When we feel defensive, when we feel a sense of "I'm right and you're wrong," we can begin to recognize the ego at work and ask ourselves:

"Do I want to be *right*, or *powerful*?"

This awareness gives us the opportunity to ignore the demands of the ego, and choose differently—to search within to determine what our authentic self truly desires.

There are some people (very few) who live without ego. So we know that it is possible. I've been close to *barely touching the surface* of this and upon grazing on the surface for short periods at a time, I felt a well of calmness that I could dip my toes into and enjoy. In this state, I would contemplate on simple things. There was quietness for short periods of time, but also, in the brief moments where ego was absent, I could be captivated by visual images from patterns on my bathroom floor. And at others times, I would make fun of ants on my kitchen floor. Seriously, I would squat down and watch the ants interact with each other and do voiceovers of what they could be thinking about and what *they could be talking about* while they went about cleaning my floor of the pieces of food that I had left behind. I even gave them names. Well, not all of them, only the awkward, wayward ones that were not following directions.

Feed your mind a good diet of happy thoughts and starve your ego.

You could starve your ego to the point of death, by removing everything that makes your identity important to you and significant others. But I will leave this guidance to the experts, those who have discovered how to live in the *absence of ego*. I can only share stories of when I barely touched the surface of this concept.

Discovering and separating your ego from your true self is one amazing first step, and it has to be a chosen by you. This is the beginning of finding your "stillness within the storm." The *storm* being the egotic life that you currently exist in—the *stillness* being choosing to simply *exist* as *you*.

Once you begin to become aware of the difference between you and your ego, there begins a discovery of reality versus our illusionary existence. This is when your subconscious begins to invade your conscious thought and the illusion that you think you are meets the resistance of your ego.

Feel *free* to *be* who you *are* without regret or fear of what others will think of you—BE YOU! This is not an easy thing to do. Because when we do this, we are opening ourselves up to rejection. By now you probably are beginning to understand that when others reject you, it's not really about you, they are really exposing what they fear the most in themselves.

When you live life understanding how your own ego works, you will understand and accept how other egos behave. Armed with this understanding, people will naturally gravitate to you and share their own stories about how they came into the understanding of who they are. These are the people that you will want to invite into your life. Fill your life with those who love you as much as you love them. Fill your body with the same goodness when you eat. Starve your ego with thoughts of cute, playful, fuzzy bunnies, kittens and puppies romping around.

When you start to let go of all the egotic elements in your life—start putting aside outside influences—you will start taking control back of your real life. The realization of the Egoticism you have been living in becomes obvious. And this helps you to understand and separate what your ego wants and what *you* really *need*.

Feed your life with love and surround yourself with people that love you as much as you love them. Fill every part of your life with people and things that inspire you. Seek what brings you happiness, both physically and mentally.

INNER MISSION

We've looked at how to discover and distance yourself from your ego. We've identified how you can recognize when your ego is at work. And we've explored what happens when the ego is discovered and how it reacts with anger, sometimes even blinding us.

Once your ego is discovered, recognized and called out into the open, it knows that its days of directing your life and feeding on whatever it desires, are soon coming to an end.

Yes, the ego's days are numbered. Your ego may have to take second "stage" to what is rising up.

The "rising up" I am talking about is *you*.

Now, let's begin to identify our daily negative self-talk. Pay attention to the negative things you say to yourself each day and begin to question if these things are really true.

Your mission?

Create two columns in your journal, one for positive thoughts and one for negative thoughts. Then, document each negative and positive thought you have during the day. Review these entries weekly, write about your discoveries, and then release the negative ones back into the universe with fire as was mentioned before.

The goal is to slowly eliminate your negative thoughts while increasing your positive thoughts.

Stillness For Thought:

Why is it so much easier for us to believe, that we are stupid and ugly people living in a world of smart and beautiful people? And who is defining and the ideal of smart and beautiful people and who is promoting it? What if *you* get to decide what is smart and beautiful?

Chapter 23

Change your thoughts, change your life

We are comprised of universal energy. Born of it, created from it, and exist in it. It is all around us, penetrating every atom that is creation, resonating within our world. When resonating atoms have the same frequencies and harmonics, an attraction is made. Good or bad, this is the law of attraction.

The universal law of attraction states: *"That what is like, attracts the same."*

Even in the life we live directed by the ego, this is true. And yet we don't see it, or recognize it. Sometimes it appears as a series of unfortunate events. Sometimes it can appear to us as fate or even as a miracle. The focus of our thoughts can change our resonance, and attract the likeness of that resonance, good or bad.

If you think that you will always be falling behind at work and never catch up, you will be. If you think no one will ever love you, no one will. If you think you will be late for an appointment, you will be.

Or, if you believe you are great at your job, you will be. If you believe that you were meant to live close to palm trees and smell the ocean from your porch, you will. If you believe that your friends love you and want to be a part of your life, they will.

But also understand that what you focus on and believe is not something you get immediately, like a wish granted from a genie. Just as we understand when life is difficult to endure—that in time *this too shall pass*—what we focus on and believe we *desire* in our lives: *this too shall **be***.

As with all matter, everything resonates. We are a collective of resonating atoms harmonizing within the space that is all around us. The law of attraction influences every part of our life—from always feeling sick and miserable, to finding our soul mate. What you continually tell yourself and others is the key. This affirmation of what you want and desire (both positive and negative) is causative to what shows up in your life.

What you say aloud, what you say within your internal thoughts, in time, will become what you say it will be.

Final Thoughts

We are what we are, and it is what it is. We have to learn to accept the things we can't change and accept who and what we are. Not only do our thoughts create our reality, our thoughts also *prevent* our "stillness" and fuel the "storm."

My hope with this book is that the movement from *who you **think** you are* to the awareness of *who you really are* has gained momentum for you. Only time will tell.

So, ***where do we go from here?***

In this huge universe, there are many things we do not completely understand. But, we don't need to, to benefit from them.

If a situation "is what it is," maybe we should just allow it to exist and take it from there.

Unconditional love resides in our unconscious, whereas anger resides in our consciousness and is fueled by emotion. The ego only has control over our consciousness. This is why we can demonstrate acts of valor, and strength, from who we really are, which resides within us untouched by outside elements.

As a society, we write the rules to live by. As a whole, we reinforce what is to be believed to be good and what is believed to be bad. But, we all intrinsically know what is truly good or bad. We've always known the truth, we just choose to ignore this *knowing* in favor of alignment with our ego.

Now that you've begun the journey to a life of understanding your ego and how it affects how you move about your life—where the *storm* starts to *move around you and not through you*—hold close those people who inspire a sense of wonder, joy, and unconditional love. Allow relationships to flourish even if it seems unconventional to you. It's not an "accident" for these people to show up in your life. Keep them close to your heart, as I'm sure they feel the same.

Physically limit your access to the media and the news. Live close to your work and places where you shop—within walking distance is ideal. Design your daily life to be as simple as possible. Rather than spending your time figuring out how you are going to schedule everything to fit into your day, simplify and allow yourself time to discover and engage in what is important to you.

Create an amicable relationship with your ego. Let it run out on its leash from time to time. Be responsible. Both you and your ego need to come to terms with social responsibility.

We can feel panicky and overwhelmed when new difficult situations arise. But, take comfort in the historical evidence which demonstrates that you have overcome all of the challenges you were faced with in the past and that they have brought you here today alive and still kicking! Remember how unimportant the past is. The future is unwritten. The only thing that really matters **is where you are right now when this moment changes to the next.**

ENDING NOTE

This book was on my bucket list.

Throughout most of my life in one way or another, I was writing about life and its meaning. In my early twenties, life for me was a value system of recognized achievements. As my life progressed with marriage and children, the previous value system was no longer valid. Early in mid-life I took business management courses through a local community college and focused on leadership—which lead me to my fascination with communication. This is where I was *awakened*. I discovered that interacting and interaction between all of us was vital. This information was cooking in a crockpot of brewing thoughts for quite some time, until now. And "Stillness within the Storm" is its result.

In the past, I have lost various chapters of my writing for so many reasons I cannot count. Over time, the content of my writing leading me in one direction or another. But what finally focused me was discovering the name of this book. All my life I was learning, discovering, and writing, but up until recently, there was no direction. No way to collate my writings and focus them in one direction, until now. This serves as a reminder to both you and me to continue doing what we love and leave the timing up to the Universe.

Helping others understand the message you aspire to get across can be challenging. I realized when I was writing that I didn't want to preach to others. I didn't want them to learn from my mistakes. I didn't want them to go through what I went through. No ... What I really wanted is for those who read this book to discover within themselves something that they could connect with and discover new beginnings within. I want others to have faith in themselves and trust in their gut feeling of what is right and follow it.

My hope is that you—the reader—will take what you've gleaned from this book to the next level. Whatever that next level may be for you. Also, I ask, that you share what you have learned with others—ask them the same questions that I have asked of you, and if you find value from reading this book, share it with others—*share the good news.*

On another note:

I've been asked to give the people that are reading my book a reference for further learning on the concepts I've shared. Here is one significant place of wonder, whose purpose for existence is to share ideas with the world. To my readers, I give you "TED"... www.**ted**.com

TED *(**T**echnology-**E**ntertainment-**D**esign) is a nonprofit devoted to ideas worth spreading; ideas usually in the form of short, powerful talks (18 minutes or less). TED began in 1984 as a conference where Technology, Entertainment, and Design converged, and today covers almost all topics—from science to business to global issues—in more than 100 languages. Meanwhile, independently run TEDx events help share ideas in communities around the world.*

About the Author

Matthew Tolleth, Writer, Author, Artist, Explorer and wine connoisseur. He resides in the Greater Seattle area with his fiancé, Julie. Both veterans; He served in the Navy and Julie served in the Air Force. They both highly value family and enjoy vacationing in beach locations and spending time with their grown children.

www.ingramcontent.com/pod-product-compliance
Lightning Source LLC
Chambersburg PA
CBHW071459070426
42452CB00041B/1941